"*The High Potential's Advantage* delivers actionable insights into the murky territory of how companies identify their highest-potential employees. You'll discover concrete ways to chart a career course and differentiate yourself. I highly recommend this book!"

> —**G. JOYCE ROWLAND,** Senior Vice President, Chief Human Resources and Administrative Officer, Sempra Energy

"*The High Potential's Advantage* is a one-of-a-kind, inside look at what it takes to become tomorrow's executive or even the CEO. I now have the essential how-to guide to succeed not only in my current role but over my entire career."

> —**DON SWAN,** Private Equity Analyst, Skyview Capital LLC

"A compelling, comprehensive guide to what it takes to become and stay a high potential. The authors' deep expertise in the field of leadership development comes through with real humility grounded in rich, practical how tos. Their engaging ability to teach through storytelling brings the insights to life."

> —**BRENDAN J. SWORDS,** Chairman and CEO, Wellington Management Company

THE HIGH POTENTIAL'S ADVANTAGE

GET NOTICED, IMPRESS YOUR BOSSES, AND BECOME A TOP LEADER

THE HIGH POTENTIAL'S ADVANTAGE

GET NOTICED, IMPRESS YOUR BOSSES, AND BECOME A TOP LEADER

Jay A. Conger
Allan H. Church

HARVARD BUSINESS REVIEW PRESS

Boston, Massachusetts

The web addresses referenced in this book were live and correct at the time of the
book's publication but may be subject to change.

Library of Congress Cataloging-in-Publication Data

Names: Conger, Jay Alden, author. | Church, Allan H., 1966- author.
Title: The high potential's advantage : get noticed, impress your bosses, and become
    a top leader / by Jay A. Conger and Allan H. Church.
Description: Boston, Massachusetts : Harvard Business Review Press, [2018]
Identifiers: LCCN 2017027847 | ISBN 9781633692886 (hardcover : alk. paper)
Subjects: LCSH: Success in business. | Leadership. | Successful people. | Executive
    coaching. | Corporate culture.
Classification: LCC HF5386 .C7454 2018 | DDC 658.4/092—dc23 LC record avail-
    able at https://lccn.loc.gov/2017027847

The paper used in this publication meets the requirements of the American National
Standard for Permanence of Paper for Publications and Documents in Libraries and
Archives Z39.48-1992.

ISBN: 978-1-63369-288-6
eISBN: 978-1-63369-289-3

To Nathan and Zoe: May you reach all of your potential in life.
—Love your Dad
To Janine for her guidance, feedback, coaching, and inspiration all these
years, which have helped me realize my potential.
—Allan

Contents

PART ONE

The Five X Factors of High-Potential Talent

PART TWO

How to Navigate Your Organization's High-Potential Processes

1

What Does It Mean to Be a High Potential and How Can You Become One?

You are ambitious. You know you have tremendous untapped potential. You dream of becoming an executive officer one day or, more boldly, a CEO. You often find yourself restless when it comes to work—wanting bigger, more rewarding, and challenging assignments. Most importantly, you want to be an influential leader who makes a genuine difference, a person who people admire and are excited to follow. You want to be one of your organization's high-potential leaders—someone people see as able to advance to much higher levels. If this description fits you, then we have a road map for arriving at your dream destination.

Our goal is to answer the destination questions on your mind as an aspiring leader. For example, you might be asking yourself: What will it take on my part to get to the senior-most levels of my organization? What skills, abilities, and knowledge do I need to get there, and do they differ at career stages or stay basically the same throughout my career? Am I better off staying in my current organization or jumping around to improve my chances of climbing the corporate ladder? What does my boss look for when assessing whether I am a high-potential leader? And what's my organization's process for assessing my potential? Should I aggressively campaign and ask for that promotion, or just put my head down and do my job the best I can . . . hoping for a promotion soon? How will I know if I've achieved high-potential status when executives in my organization don't share that information?

If you have these questions, then we have the answers—whether you are just entering the workforce, brand-new to your organization, a midcareer professional, or a junior executive thinking about how to get to that ultimate level of CEO, CFO, or COO. We design and implement high-potential identification processes in well-known global organizations. We have coached, observed, and assessed thousands of front-line and middle managers as well as senior executives. For this book, we interviewed over a hundred leaders along with dozens of senior HR officers who oversee the high-potential talent of their organizations. We also dived deep into the research about high-potential leaders and why they sometimes derail their careers (see the sidebar "The Research Behind This Book" near the end of this chapter).

Our core finding—and the key insight of this book—is that five critical skills differentiate high potentials from everyone else. We call them the *X factors of high potential*. Anyone can learn and get better at these skills, but our research shows that you must be proficient in all five to get on your company's high-potential list. And you must always be improving them to *stay* on the list. Certain skills are building blocks to others, so we'll describe the sequence in which you need to cultivate each.

In *The High Potential's Advantage*, we examine in depth each of the five X factors—what each one is, how each works, and how to develop that particular skill. We will also take you behind the scenes to understand how bosses and organizations determine whether you deserve that high-potential status. You will learn about the mechanics and politics of the processes that your company uses to assess your potential.

Our aim throughout this book is straightforward—to help you become an influential icon in your organization and ultimately to build a great career. No matter your career or industry, you will find this book a valuable reference. Its insights are the product of our research looking across the broadest spectrum of high-potential designations, from early career to senior management, and our collective experience designing and working with high-potential programs in many different industries.

But first, you're probably wondering what exactly is a "high potential"—and why you should care.

How Organizations Define High Potential

We like the following succinct definition from one organization: "A highly valuable contributor with a great deal of stretch capability within the organization. Such individuals are typically promoted to higher levels beyond their current role, and a select few can be seen as leading the organization at the senior levels."[1] Many organizations—and likely yours—define high potential as concretely as "your capacity to step into a role that is *two levels or more above the one you currently hold.*"

If performance is all about delivering results in your current job, then potential is simply about the opportunity to deliver results in leadership roles in the future. Most of us want to perform well and be recognized for our efforts. Companies know this well and have pay-for-performance philosophies and systems to support this mindset. But companies need more from their leaders than just top-notch performance now. They are hungry for talent that can rapidly grow into demanding roles later. So they proactively assess your potential for jobs that are several *levels* above your current one. The question they ask before they decide on your next promotion is a simple one: "Do you have the right stuff to rapidly learn and lead in a job that is far more complex and demanding than the one you currently hold?" We are going to help you to ensure that the answer is always yes.

Only a small pool of individuals makes it to this talent designation. Our research with hundreds of organizations shows that typically only 10 percent to 15 percent of an organization's overall talent comprise that pool.

Why Being Designated a High Potential Really Matters

The real reason you'll want to strive for the designation as high-potential talent is that, once you are chosen, entirely new opportunities open up. Organizations invest their scarce development resources most heavily in their top-rated talent. The logic is straightforward. So the smartest choice is to invest those limited dollars and opportunities in individuals with the absolute greatest potential.

What specific kinds of exciting opportunities can you expect as a high-potential leader, ones that your peers may not get a shot at? The following are the major ones:

Accelerated promotions. Companies focus on pulling high potentials through the organization quickly, which translates into faster advancement up the corporate ladder than anyone else. Just as importantly, research on these high-flyer leaders indicates that they often maximize their learning in new roles after about eighteen months on the job. So if you are a high potential, you are likely to move into new roles faster than your peers.

More frequent and diverse roles. Along with faster advancement, high potentials have more opportunities to build their knowledge of the business and their leadership muscle. If your company assessed you as high-potential talent, it will ask you to change jobs more frequently and consider you for more critical experiences, key roles, or one-of-a-kind high-visibility projects than your peers. One promising twenty-four-year-old we know is already in her third job in the same organization.

Sometimes, frequent job changes are about testing your leadership fortitude. The CEO might invite you to join a special task force to build out a strategic plan for a new product line or to head up a joint venture. You might become part of the due diligence team considering a large acquisition project. In organizations with a significant multinational footprint—where a global mindset and experience in different countries are prerequisites for a top leadership position—you could be tapped for significant international travel and assignments. Best of all, your company manages your career more thoughtfully, ensuring accelerated development opportunities that your colleagues may never experience.

More development resources and support. High potentials almost always have priority for more of the company's development resources than their peers. In one study we conducted, 50 percent of the participating global corporations focused their talent investments primarily on high-potential leaders.[2] This means that you will be the first to be involved in internal leadership programs, mentoring relationships, external course offerings, special projects, coaching support, feedback and assessment processes, and other developmental opportunities. While some individuals might complain that these are extra demands on their time (rarely do companies remove your current role's responsibilities so you can participate in these activities), your good-natured acceptance of them will indicate your high-potential nature. If you decide to opt out of them, you will send a signal to your organization that you don't want to be considered high-potential talent.

Visibility to senior leadership. Finally, being a high potential means you likely have far greater opportunities to meet, spend time with, and even work directly with the executive leaders in your organization. You might meet them through special task forces, mentoring relationships, invitations to present where you normally might not, participation in a leadership program where executives are leading or speaking, or simply having breakfast or lunch with a senior leader in what are called "meet and greets."

In many cases, your CEO might know who you are. Indeed, she is likely to have your name and talent data at her fingertips.

When she meets you, she has already seen your performance history, educational background, prior roles, and previous employers. She is likely to know your leadership and functional strengths, career preferences, assessment results, mobility preferences, and so on. While she will use this information to plan for your career during talent reviews (a topic we discuss at length in chapter 8), this heightened visibility means that you have to stay on top of your game. You have to keep earning your special status.

How Will I Know When I Am Considered High-Potential Talent?

Many organizations don't actually tell their people straight out that they are considered high-potential talent. If you work for a large organization, your firm probably has a high-potential talent pool, whether you know it or not. An estimated 40 to 60 percent of the firms using these designations will not officially tell you. In one of our studies, we discovered 66 percent of some of the largest companies in the world did not formally share high-potential status with their designates.[3]

The Debate on Whether to Tell You about Your High-Potential Status

A big debate among senior leaders in organizations is going on about whether to inform you of your status. Some argue for hiding the designation from you. Surprisingly enough, advocates actually have some compelling reasons. They worry that not receiving the designation might demotivate you. Your organization's culture may also place a premium on collaboration and teamwork, and your boss may be reluctant to go public with high-potential designations because it could encourage too much internal competition and upset healthy working relationships. Or, superiors simply don't want to raise your expectations about fast-track promotions or more frequent or bigger pay increases. They are also concerned about inflating your ego. In addition, some organizations like to take calculated risks with individuals who sit on the borderline of high potential status. They want to test their speculations but need the next assignment to validate them. If designations were public, they'd be less inclined to make these borderline bets.

Those on the other side—the ones who want you to know you're a high potential—have equally compelling arguments. First, the designation is a terrific reward, so it should be visible. Transparency should motivate more individuals to work harder for that recognition. Just receiving the designation should further fuel your motivation. After all, more opportunities lie ahead if you continue to excel. Second, you'd be less tempted to leave for another organization if you know that you are on the fast track. Finally, research has shown that most young people entering the workforce value transparency. They want to join companies that are open, honest, and forthcoming about their talent programs and processes. Telling people where they really stand is a key component of that honesty and transparency, and attracts talent.

The Secret Process Organizations Use to Identify Their High Potentials

The assessment process companies use to identify high potentials is sometimes a great mystery. Throughout this book, we are going to demystify what goes on inside this black box. You'll develop a deep appreciation for what becoming and staying a high-potential leader within your organization really takes.

An entire industry has been built around the assessments and processes behind high-potential designations, with annual expenditures in the billions of dollars. While we can trace the origins of assessment to practices in ancient China and Greece, the tools organizations now use emerged in the twentieth century. What started as a means for identifying the best people for leadership roles in the military was quickly adopted in the 1960s in the form of assessment centers at companies like AT&T. Over the years, the types and numbers of tools have blossomed.

Literally hundreds of management consultants, search (recruiting) firms, and psychological groups offering tests, surveys, and simulations have designed ways to measure your ability to perform at high levels. These measures of high potential include everything from cognitive tests (for example, how smart you are), personality measures (your disposition and possible derailments), 360-degree feedback assessments (the behaviors you demonstrate to others in the workplace), and live assessment centers or online simulations (your knowledge, judgment, and decisions in different scenarios). Although all these tools have their strengths and limitations (we discuss how best to prepare for these later in the book), the point is that, in today's employment landscape, it is hard to avoid the high-potential assessment machine.

Figuring Out Your Status

So what should you do if your organization doesn't tell you where you stand? You still want to know what it thinks of you, don't you? You could ask outright. If that doesn't work, look for signs that strongly suggest you are already in the high-potential talent pool. We've outlined some of the more common indicators in the sidebar "You Might Already Be in the High-Potential Pool."

If several of the indicators in the sidebar describe your situation, you are likely already considered high-potential talent. Your challenge then is to ensure that you *stay* a high potential. Once you're in, there is no guarantee you'll stay in. Companies usually review the status of their high potentials annually, just to see whether they continue to deserve the designation. In some companies, this refresh process is part of their standard, ongoing talent management review. Later in this book, we'll share in greater depth how and why high potentials lose their status, and how to avoid these pitfalls in your own career.

YOU MIGHT ALREADY BE IN THE HIGH-POTENTIAL POOL

Look at the following list to see which items describe your situation at work. The more that you check off, the more likely you already possess a high-potential designation. At the very least, you are on the road to that status.

- You consistently receive glowing performance reviews, and when the company hands out bonuses or long-term incentives, you get your fair share or more than others.

- You get first crack at new projects and task forces before your colleagues are asked to join them.

- You have frequent conversations and check-ins with your manager, managers' manager, and HR about how you are doing and what's next for you. You are already planning for your next role twelve months into your current one, and people are listening to you (you're not just talking to yourself) and responding positively about what you want.

- You are invited to participate in leadership development programs with informative speakers held at impressive locations and hotels.

- You are scheduled for breakfast, lunch, or dinner meetings with senior executives, board directors, senior HR leaders, or your CEO when they are in town. You are invited to participate in formal assessment and development programs that include survey tools and measurements and perhaps even working with an executive coach to help you with your feedback and development plan.

- You have more and more responsibilities added to your current role to help you develop new capabilities.

- You continue to be tested with tough projects and assignments.

The Problem with Defining Someone's Potential—and Why This Gives You Power to Influence It

Another problem—and one of the primary reasons we wrote this book—is that the process of gauging someone's potential is elusive and imprecise— and highly subjective. It involves determining how well you *will perform in future jobs that you have never had and with demands that you have never experienced.* Most bosses simply look to see how well you are doing *now* to determine your potential (in the sidebar "Why Assessing Potential Is a Crapshoot," we offer some thoughts on why assessing anyone's potential is a crapshoot, especially for a boss). Yet, research indicates that a person's current performance rarely predicts future performance.

Precisely because it's so hard for managers and organizations to truly assess someone's potential, it's something that you can influence. Our research shows that your performance on the five X factors will most influence your bosses' perceptions of whether you're ready to be considered a high potential, and each factor is within your control to develop.

Becoming and Staying a High Potential throughout Your Career

Our research shows that you can do specific things to be considered a high potential. Whatever process your organization has in place for assessing high-potential talent, we have discovered that five universal skills differentiate high potentials from everyone else. Over your career, the real high-potential differentiators, our X factors, are the secret sauce that distinguishes the high-potential leaders from their peers (see figure 1-1). Beyond your first or second promotion, the X-factor skills get you that high-potential designation and ensure you keep it. Your superiors will look for these factors when making the call about your future potential. If

FIGURE 1-1

The five X factors

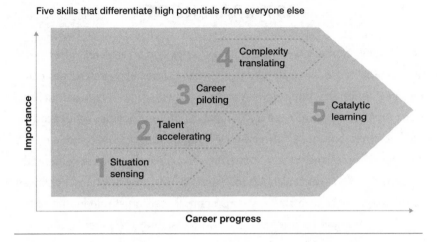

Five skills that differentiate high potentials from everyone else

you want to get ahead, you need to have these essential X factors through-out your career.

You can't change the basics of who you are (if you're simply not that strategic or don't like people, you will need to find ways to work around those foundational issues). However, these X factors don't usually show up on lists of leadership competencies or on performance review forms. They describe more holistic skills and capabilities that integrate across the more commonly used talent assessment tools. Possessing the five can help you achieve that coveted high-potential ranking and propel you to that status in a wide range of organizational settings and roles. For example, we found that all of the X factors applied across different types of companies, industries, and levels of the hierarchy.

Most importantly, you can develop the X factors over time with con-scious effort. While your raw capabilities are important, you can cultivate the X factors throughout an entire career if you focus intently on develop-ing them. If you'd like to know how well you already stack up on the five, take the self-assessment at the end of the chapter.

You have to be good at all five skills. But, at different points in your career, some are more important than others. The first two X factors, for

WHY ASSESSING POTENTIAL IS A CRAPSHOOT

The identification of potential is both a science and an art—and often more art. Why? Because we're all human. Our own biases and preferences come into play when making judgments about others. In an organizational setting, your manager makes a determination of your abilities influenced by data from personal observations and feelings, feedback from coworkers, and even formal assessment tests. So two bosses could judge you very differently.

Consider the case of Michelle, for example. Her company hired her based on her experience as a strategy consultant. In her initial role in one of the business units, she focused primarily on translating the parent company's strategies into tangible business plans. She excelled and was labeled a high potential. Two years later, Michelle was promoted into a new role at the parent company, leading the identification of new initiatives.

Her new boss, the vice president of strategy, was very supportive at first, but within six months, she decided that Michelle didn't have what it took to be successful. Her high-potential designation was removed. In another six months, there was talk of putting Michelle on a performance plan with the possible outcome of leaving the organization (just twelve months after being designated a high potential and receiving a glowing performance review). While Michelle tried her best, there was a disconnection between her and her boss in what was expected in the role.

Then her boss and another colleague swapped roles at the vice president level. Overnight, the new VP gave Michelle a short window in which to change perceptions of her capabilities. The new VP had different needs and ways of working than the prior executive. Michelle's natural strengths and style were once again in sync with her boss. A year later, she was up for a promotion and high-potential designation.

Bosses base their judgments on what they observe about you in your current role. Yet the strengths and capacity to learn that you demonstrate so well in your present role may not be enough in the future. Another factor that makes potential difficult to accurately assess is that you are never in a steady state. You are learning and changing as you experience new job demands. You are constantly evolving. Given your learning capacity, you might have far more potential than your boss realizes. So the "potential" label is *not* absolute, as much as we'd like to think it is.

Another critical question is about your potential for what role exactly. A high-potential leader could be someone with great possibilities for filling any number of roles or a specific role, like the head of a research and development lab or the CEO. Different capabilities and expertise are needed in each of these roles in order to be highly successful.

Formal assessment tools (e.g., tests, simulations, surveys) and talent review processes can help overcome some of the biases by providing a common standard and showing managers a different side of your abilities they may not otherwise see. In the end, however, it comes down to their judgment about you. When your manager labels you a high potential, she is betting on your ability to go further in the organization based on a combination of factors. So your level of intelligence, personality preferences, motivation to do well, ability to learn from experiences, basic leadership and management skills, and your functional depth all come into an equation that results in a high-potential designation. While you can't become smarter overnight, change your personality, or significantly influence your test scores, you can do something about how your boss and others in the organization see you in the workplace. The X factors we present here are areas you can control and get significantly better at. By focusing on enhancing your skills in each of these, you can influence the process.

THE RESEARCH BEHIND THIS BOOK

We based the X factors on a comprehensive, three-pronged research approach to determining what it takes to be seen as a high potential in the workplace. Our research looks at how and where you can have the most impact in shaping your career. We began with a comprehensive literature review conducted by Silzer and Church of over fifty years of academic theory, consulting and individual assessment models, internal talent management frameworks, and research in the fields of applied psychology and organizational behavior.[4] From this review, we formulated a framework called the Leadership Potential BluePrint.[5] This outlines the key foundational, growth, and career factors that were helpful in classifying all the possible variables that have predicted whether someone is a high-potential leader.

Next, using this model as a baseline, we reviewed and integrated insights from many recent studies on high-potential talent and assessment practices conducted with over a hundred best-in-class organizations along with additional data collected on high potentials from forty-five companies regarding

example, are important skills to develop early in your career and you're unlikely to advance without them. But the further up you go, the more important the other skills are and the more opportunity you'll have to practice the third and fourth factors. The last X factor is foundational—it is the one skill that drives all the others. The following are brief descriptions of each:

- **Situation sensing.** The first X factor is the capacity to sense rapidly your boss's unique stylistic demands and priorities. With sensing capacity, you can adapt thoughtfully to what matters most to superiors. The person most likely to assess your potential is your boss. Mess up that relationship, and you'll totally miss a shot at the high-potential designation.

the distinguishing attributes of high-potential leaders.[6] The latter was published in a popular *Harvard Business Review* article "Are You a High Potential?" This research told us what companies are actually doing and how they think about the different components of potential—for example, which matter the most, which are most likely to be fixed traits, and which traits can be more easily developed. It also informed us about the attributes of high-potential talent across a broad range of organizations, roles, and levels of hierarchy.

Finally, we conducted interviews with over a hundred high-potential and highly successful leaders in a variety of organizations and functions on their perspective of what they see as enablers and derailers of potential in junior through senior talent. In addition, we interviewed three dozen senior HR leaders who oversee high-potential talent. We augmented all this information with our combined fifty years of internal assessment and development work, external consulting, and academic writing and teaching in these same topics. A synthesis of the insights we gained from the interviews, along with all the prior work done on the BluePrint and external benchmarking led us to identify the five key X factors that we present in this book.

- **Talent accelerating.** This factor is a constellation of skills related to assessing, motivating, and guiding the many teams you'll lead over your career. After your first job as an individual contributor, you'll move into team leadership roles and eventually be leading teams of teams. So you need to be a quick study of talent, and masterful in developing that talent. High potentials succeed because they are able to draw deeply on the strengths and drives of the individuals they lead. In essence, your talent is built upon the talent of your team.

- **Career piloting.** As you move up and across your organization, you'll have more challenging assignments to develop and test your potential. Each will require remarkable versatility in terms of adapting your behavior and mindset. You'll have new and complex bodies of knowledge to acquire and master. The breadth of your leadership skills will be honed and tested simultaneously. You'll discover the critical importance of being highly perceptive along with being comfortable with ambiguity, and the necessity of a calm, perceptive, and relational demeanor.

- **Complexity translating.** When you start out on your career, you'll be rewarded for your ability to gather lots of data and deeply understand an issue. As you move up, your ability to integrate and simplify these same divergent sources of information is more important. From there, you'll have to craft a compelling narrative, that is, translate complexity, for different audiences. In a later chapter, you'll see why you need to develop this essential skill.

- **Catalytic learning.** This foundational factor drives all the others. It allows you to accomplish all the other factors. Long-term high potentials are able to learn and keep learning even after establishing remarkable track records. They are deeply and broadly curious. These qualities ensure they become and stay world-class situation sensors, talent accelerators, career pilots, and complexity translators. Most importantly, they always turn their learning into insights, initiatives and actions—all aimed at improving or transforming the status quo. They are never passive. That's the catalytic part.

What to Expect in This Book

In part one, chapters 2–6, we'll share an in-depth exploration of each of the X factors and how each works to unleash potential. For example, you are going to discover which X-factor attribute entrepreneur Elon Musk and high-potential organizational leaders share. This quality keeps them constantly evolving and is a trademark quality of world-class athletes as well.

You will explore the case of a senior manager who is the number-one choice on everyone's succession list to become the highest-ranking leader in his professional services firm. You'll discover that he consistently does one activity that his peers forget to do, one of our differentiating X factors. You will learn how one high potential leveraged a company conference to reinvent his role and catapult himself into a much bigger leadership role. Again, an X factor at work.

You will find that some X factors are so crucial that, without them, you'll derail, even if you excel at all the others. We will tell the story of a high-potential manager with a fabulous, high-profile track record who fell from grace. Paradoxically, he was the highest scoring among a select group of high-potential leaders on an assessment testing his ability to be the company CEO. While he seemingly had the right stuff, he had one fatal shortcoming: He was lacking one of our crucial X factors. You'll learn what causes high-potential leaders to lose their status and how you can sidestep these common derailers.

In part two, we'll show you how to navigate your organization's high-potential process. In chapter 7, we take you behind the scenes to examine how both your boss and your organization formally assess and evaluate your potential. You will learn which types of assessment tools they commonly use to measure different traits and skills. We will also provide steps so that you can own more of the assessment process and, in turn, successfully navigate these otherwise murky waters.

In chapter 8, we'll take you inside the black box of the talent review meeting and share what senior executives talk about behind closed doors and how and when they talk about you. We'll discuss the importance of ensuring your internal résumé (often called an employee profile) is up-to-date and that your boss and your organization know exactly what you've done before and what you want to do going forward.

In chapter 9, we will discuss why you need to understand the nuances of your organization's culture and how it shapes the ways in which the X factors manifest themselves. While the underlying behaviors of the X factors are consistent, the ways in which they are brought to life in different organizations are unique, thanks to culture. You need to learn how

DO YOU HAVE THE RIGHT STUFF?

A Self-Assessment of the High-Potential X Factors

These fifteen assessment descriptions are designed so you can quickly gauge your future potential. See how many of them describe you. The more that do, the more likely you have the right stuff to become high-potential talent. This self-assessment will also help you to see which X factors should be your development priorities. How many of these describe the way you work?

Situation sensing

☐ You are perceptive in reading your bosses' performance demands and in turn are able to consistently work to help them achieve their agendas.

☐ You are interpersonally savvy and observant. As a result, you are highly adaptable and can easily flex your work style to meet the stylistic needs of different types of bosses.

☐ You enjoy taking initiative and following through, and you are always looking out for ways to solve organizational problems and capture opportunities, even when they are not part of your job's responsibilities.

Talent accelerating

☐ You are manically focused on spotting and shepherding exceptionally talented people wherever they may be and then building the best possible teams with this talent.

☐ You are dedicated to the development of your team members, while constantly seeking to improve your own skills as a leader.

☐ You act quickly to deal with those people who aren't meeting performance expectations.

Career piloting

- ❏ You are an experience junkie and thrive on taking on new challenges and assignments even when these result in an unpredictable career path.

- ❏ You approach new opportunities with an extreme openness and tolerance for ambiguity about how you will navigate the situation.

- ❏ You are a calming influence on those around you in times of pressure, stress, and change, helping yourself and others to adapt to changing circumstances thoughtfully and appropriately.

Complexity translating

- ❏ You are a "data native" who thinks broadly about all kinds of information and sees data and patterns everywhere.

- ❏ You are a wiz at connecting the dots for others by turning analytics into actionable insights.

- ❏ You are a persuasive storyteller using compelling narratives to communicate decisively and influence others at all levels to follow an agenda.

Catalytic learning

- ❏ You are incessantly curious and enjoy learning about what is happening in the world around you and how you might apply that information.

- ❏ You are naturally self-reflective and versatile, always looking for ways to improve your own capabilities and knowledge as a leader.

- ❏ You take an optimistic and proactive approach to the future and how and where you can make an impact.

to read the signs of your company's culture and how best to demonstrate your skills and abilities in any given setting. We'll also help you uncover the cultural pitfalls to avoid.

. . .

Our book is about taking charge of your future. We have a singular goal— to ensure not only that you achieve the icon status of a high-potential leader, but more importantly, that you have a deeply rewarding career— one that harnesses your fullest potential as a leader. Welcome to your high-potential journey.

PART ONE

The Five X Factors of High-Potential Talent

2

Situation Sensing

How to Build Trust with Your Bosses

The first X factor has to do with your most important relationship at work—the one with your boss. Other relationships matter, too, and we'll explore more of them in the next chapter, but this one truly stands out. Especially at the earlier stages of your career—where this X-factor skill is disproportionately more important than the others—only your bosses know you, judge you, and represent you to the organization. In the meetings where executives confer high-potential status, your boss must go to bat for you. A high-potential talent designation is therefore all about *advocacy*.

Think of your potential as an extension of that of your bosses, often tied to their own advancement and rewards. To be your advocate, they must have compelling evidence that you are substantially furthering *their* agenda. Impressing bosses in memorable and unique ways is the key to becoming high-potential talent. More importantly, if they trust you, they will want to see you develop and succeed. You'll end up creating a virtuous cycle for yourself, with your boss looking out for you.

First, your immediate mission is to have your bosses think of you as:

- A top performer now

- Someone they can trust deeply to further their highest priorities

- An individual with great potential to grow, whatever that means in the eyes of your boss and your organization

Situation sensing is a critical skill to master early in your career because what one person in the organization considers important could be very different from what's important to someone else. You have to be able to figure that out and act accordingly. You will only succeed if you are doing the right things extremely well, in the eyes of your bosses. This skill is all about sensing the agendas, high-stakes demands, and style imperatives of your boss and quickly addressing them in appropriate ways. Your first order of business is to figure out your bosses and what you need to do to create the right relationship with them.

Your Job Number One: Sensing and Flexing with Every Boss

Becoming masterful at situation sensing provides you a twofold advantage. One, it gives you an adaptive edge, and second, bosses see the skill as one indicator of high-potential talent. In the animal kingdom, a few creatures adapt to the environment that surrounds them by changing colors or slowing down or speeding up their metabolism to ensure they flourish in any situation. For you, situation sensing means observing and responding to the task priorities, work styles, habits, and behaviors that your boss values most. In some cases, this might mean only slightly shifting your behavior and ways of working. In other cases, you might need to work in a totally different way than you are accustomed to and that has so far ensured your success. That said, we don't want you to kowtow to your boss or become a sycophant. You'll end up losing the respect of your colleagues and your self-esteem. We'll say more about this in our discussion of what to do with bad or unethical bosses.

So, here's your challenge. You have to flex with every new boss. Why? Each boss is truly unique. The many bosses you have now and in the future have different priorities, styles, political realities, and aspirations. The approach that worked so well with your last boss is unlikely to succeed with the next. It could even backfire. This is why you can easily gain and lose a high-potential designation in a transition to a new boss. You have to impress each one, consistently, quickly, and across the variety of contexts in which you'll be working. Your track record to date is no insurance policy against work and stylistic misfits with a boss.

As a result, "boss sensing" has to occur at all levels and stages in a career. But even as you demonstrate this skill early on and as you progress upward in your organization, your situation sensing has to become more expansive and elevated. At the director level, you have to read your boss's boss and your boss's peers. Knowing the key players in the hierarchy and what differs about each is a high-potential differentiator. At the highest levels, like your CEO's, you deal with a board of directors and powerful external stakeholders (e.g., investors, regulatory agents, governments, unions, etc.). Imagine the complexity of reading all of their agendas and being able to flex stylistically across them. You can begin to see why this skill of sensing is so important to cultivate.

In this chapter, we start by examining the key areas where you must demonstrate outstanding performance to your boss. Specifically, you have *four opportunity zones* to prove yourself—where you can show that you are already thinking at your boss's level and can even take on aspects of your boss's job. We discuss them in order of importance. Of course, your approach to these tasks has to be seen as wholehearted support for your bosses and their success. This should not be perceived as stepping on their toes or as acts of contrived ingratiation. We show you how to tackle each opportunity zone successfully to boost your boss's favorable impressions of your potential.

Next, we turn to how you need to adapt to the *work habit demands* of your boss. For example, each boss you'll encounter believes in certain style imperatives, rightly or wrongly: "This is what it takes to be an effective leader." These style assumptions are so firmly entrenched in their beliefs that you'd be hard-pressed to persuade your bosses to the contrary.

Detecting and mirroring them in your own actions are critical to your success. We will discuss how to determine your boss's style imperatives and adapt to them.

This chapter closes with a discussion of what to do when you have a bad and/or unethical boss. These situations can seriously jeopardize your status as a high potential, and you need to prepare for them. We'll explain how.

The Four Zones of Opportunity

Situation sensing your boss is about doing four things:

1. Determining which tasks will help propel your boss's success

2. Tackling every assignment as if you are already at the level of your boss or boss's boss

3. Demonstrating initiative beyond expectations that solves an emerging organizational challenge

4. Taking work off your boss's plate

Here's how you should approach each one.

Make the Signature Tasks of Your Boss Your Highest Priority

To differentiate yourself, you'll have to sense exceptionally well your boss's expectations around tasks, the hardest and most important part of situation sensing. Your dilemma is that your time and energy are limited, and as a high potential, you have a heavier workload. So you have to be very strategic about the degree to which you invest in the many tasks you have on your plate. A simple way to think about how to best allocate your time is to first determine which assignments are about core essential tasks that need to be completed but are not critical. Perform well on these, but don't overinvest your time and energy in them.

More important are your boss's highest-priority projects. Across the broad range of your responsibilities are likely to be anywhere from two to four tasks that your boss highly values. We call these the "signature tasks." They become distinguishing career accomplishments for which you both will be known and recognized. You can easily identify them because your boss and other leaders in your organization give them a disproportionate amount of attention. Your boss asks about them frequently. They may take up significant time in meetings. Your boss will be particularly impatient about their progress. Bosses praise or criticize the people who are working most directly on these tasks and tend to put the best or most valued people on them.

The optimal way to discern signature tasks is to ask your boss directly what they are, especially when you are setting your goals for the year. Once you know the signature tasks, you must continually revisit them as your boss asks you to do other things. Your risk will be that new assignments could divert your focus from these signature tasks. So ongoing prioritization with your boss is key. You must also bring a clear point of view about what to deprioritize among your other tasks so you stay focused on the signature ones. Make your boss part of this deprioritization decision and therefore partially accountable for complaints about tasks or projects that suddenly become lower priorities.

Know these signature tasks cold and excel at them. The key point is that the boss comes to trust you and your capabilities. She literally says to herself, "I can trust you to help both myself and our organization achieve our most pressing goals." How you achieve the outcomes can sometimes carry more weight in your boss's eyes. For example, being overly directive and authoritarian—what we might call "scorched earth" tactics—to achieve signature tasks will end up derailing you in some organizations. In others, moving too slowly and relying excessively on consensus building will derail you. (We'll discuss these stylistic and cultural dimensions in depth in chapter 9.)

When performance outcomes are below expectations on the signature tasks, you must handle such difficult situations with integrity, unselfishness, and hard work. Exhibiting these traits will counterbalance the disappointing results in your boss's eyes. Make sure your boss has been engaged all along the way in your decisions. In particular, keep her updated on your challenges and, if appropriate, involve her in the resolution. Some bosses will even ask you point blank, "What can I do to help you?" This is code for which problems can she fix for you or what barriers can she tackle that might be above your pay grade but must be overcome to successfully deliver the signature task. It will help if things don't work out as planned if your boss knows you did everything in your power to be successful and that you engaged her when needed. Remember to be strategic when you take advantage of her assistance.

How do you determine which tasks are core and which are signature? A list of characteristics in the sidebar "Core versus Signature Tasks: What's the Difference?" shows how we differentiate between the two types of tasks. Use your observational powers and ask directly (for example, you could ask your boss what he is working on for his boss) to determine the highest priority or most important business goals for the year. Many companies have formal performance management systems that provide visibility to the boss's key objectives. If your boss formally cascades his objectives to you (a common practice), make sure you have figured out the appropriate weighting for yours.

Perform Every Task As If You're at a Higher Level

Reflecting on his high-potential direct report, Wade, a senior manager, explained how to find your next opportunity zone for high-potential status:

> I have three managers who report to me. One is average, and
> the other two are exceptional. But of the latter two, one has this
> ability to think and act broadly. He is the one that is visibly mak-
> ing my organization stronger. The other high performer is really
> knowledgeable, strong in managing the costs and environmental
> demands of our operations. I sleep well at night thanks to him. But
> here is the catch—his ability to contribute more broadly is limited.

I moved him into a bigger role to test him, and he learned a lot but achieved nothing exceptional in his performance. So I put him back into his prior role. Now the truly exceptional performer is my director for customer service. He says to himself, "I want to build a world-class customer service function." He is the person who has the highest potential . . . He is creating a multiplier effect through his team. He is building a deeper, stronger team than his predecessor. He is very good at helping people understand how the collective work of our organization fits into the larger organization. He does this by sharing information broadly, helping people develop a sense of aspirational purpose that energizes them and making them feel bigger at their individual jobs. The most successful folks think about their responsibility in *the context of the broader enterprise* . . . from the perspective of my boss and my boss's boss. They are acting with a mindset that is one or more levels above their job.

The second opportunity zone is a key indicator that bosses look for in a high potential—whether you are performing your tasks from the perspective of someone in the next level up. How do you do that? Start by framing your assignments through the lens that your boss uses to make his or her own decisions. For example, let's say you are working in operations, and your primary role (core task) is to ensure that the five production lines manufacturing gourmet chocolate bark cookies under your watch are running smoothly and on time. When the challenge comes to deliver a larger than anticipated order to a key customer, what do you do? A solid performer would determine how best to reprioritize the schedule and perhaps add some additional shifts to get the job done for the customer. Afterward, the solid performer would return operations to normal production.

The high potential, however, would recognize that this might be a bigger opportunity and, in turn, would consider the larger context and take a more far-reaching approach. Perhaps this customer will repeat the request or perhaps this indicates increased demand overall. Either way, the high potential would rethink the entire manufacturing process end to end and identify those areas that will result in lasting increased capacity,

CORE VERSUS SIGNATURE TASKS: WHAT'S THE DIFFERENCE?

Core tasks

- Are routine, repeatable, or occurring continuously

- Support the delivery of an existing process or program

- Include well-documented tasks that have a history of consistent execution

- Maintain strong relationships with existing clients, customers, providers, and other key stakeholders

- Deliver outcomes such as reports, documentation, analyses, or budgets, and so on

- Reflect standard continuous improvement efforts focused on important but incremental enhancements

- Manage an ongoing team while retaining existing levels of engagement, productivity, and talent

- Deliver primary objectives against predetermined targets (particularly when those targets do not reflect "stretch" goals)

Signature tasks

- Connect directly to your boss's top priorities

- Are highly visible to the organization through measurable outcomes

---

while still meeting the customer's needs in the short term. She most likely would find a way to engage with the customer on her own to gather some additional data. In the end, she'd successfully pitch to her superiors the need for additional resources and a rejiggering of production. By doing so, she has shown the ability to take on the perspective of more senior operations leadership where the future of the business, not just her individual performance goals, is in her scope of vision.

- Develop new, unique, or innovative ideas or concepts

- Implement and deliver new products, processes, or programs

- Lead to the overhaul, evaluation, turnaround, or redesign of an existing process with the aim of taking it to the next level

- Address critical and difficult challenges associated with a new or existing client, customer, or stakeholder (e.g., obtaining a new key account, saving one that was going poorly, solving a major public relations issue, responding to a significant crisis)

- Lead a major change to the enterprise itself (e.g., merger, acquisition, divestiture, reorganization, etc.)

- Guide a team or organization through a major transformation with a significant impact on employee engagement, performance, or talent

- Are highly important to the CEO or to a top executive's career legacy

- Will directly affect the company's brand or reputation and are highly visible

- Entail a high risk of failure, embarrassment, or loss of money, or significant upside potential for success, pride, and profit for the organization

How do you best cultivate the vantage point of your bosses and their bosses as you undertake an assignment? The sidebar "Thinking at Levels above Your Own" describes the types of questions your superiors likely ask themselves when it comes to this broader perspective. It often involves assuming a more strategic viewpoint about customers, shareholders, trends, threats, and opportunities in your industry. Think through what can go wrong as well as right and the impact on the critical stakeholders.

When you are assigned a critical task, solve for the bigger issue of which this assignment is just one component. If you possess this deep, big-picture knowledge, you have a far higher probability of being promoted to executive roles. Without it, you'll find yourself locked out.

Demonstrate Unexpected and Exceptional Initiative beyond the Signature Tasks

The third opportunity zone for building trust with your boss is to undertake voluntarily an initiative beyond the boundaries of your responsibilities—one that visibly improves the organization's effectiveness or exemplifies a core value. These initiatives call attention to you as an individual with unique talents or entrepreneurial spirit or else a leader with strong and admirable standards. For example, Ray Bennett, Chief Global Officer, Global Operations at Marriott International, explained how, in his early career, he drew attention to his potential through the store displays he created for his then-employer, PepsiCo:

> I was a sales representative. My job was to visit grocery stores early in the morning and write up product orders for the next day. My associates would show up at 3:30 in the morning to fill up the shelves. So I would arrive at the same time and help them put the actual product on the shelf and make the displays. I started to spin every can and bottle so that their facings produced a giant Pepsi billboard. It made an amazing impression on the store customers as they walked into the soda aisle. A few months into my job, the regional manager toured my stores. He told my boss that he wanted to speak to me. When we met, he said to me: "Your stores are so unique because of the displays you've created with the can facings. You are the first person I've ever seen do this. How did you get your associates to do that?" I told him that I wanted us to be an exceptional team and that displays were one part of that goal. He asked me what I wanted to do career-wise? I told him that I wanted to be an executive. He told me to keep doing what I was doing, and I'd get there.

THINKING AT LEVELS ABOVE YOUR OWN

How can you practice thinking at levels above you? What does exceptional performance look like from your boss's vantage point? Begin by considering the following questions as you weigh how to best undertake each assignment:

- How does performance on this task directly influence the broader business goals—the ones my superiors have to address? In what ways could it be accomplished to further the strategic, organizational, or shareholder agendas of my firm?

- Beyond my own work group, what other key stakeholders, processes, and policies have an impact on the outcome of this task beyond my immediate decisions? How can I best learn and incorporate these vantage points into my approach?

- Which stakeholders are supporting, neutral, or working at cross-purposes to my goals? Who do I need to win over? Who could act as my ambassadors to influence other stakeholders on my behalf?

- If I were running the business unit or even my company, what changes would I make in order to enhance the outcome of this task? What would I preserve or incrementally refine because these existing approaches have been foundational to our success to date?

- What building-block leadership competencies do I need to start developing now if I wish to lead at the level of my boss's boss or even my CEO's? What skills do they frequently leverage in their roles that I have not yet fully developed or simply lack?

- What functional perspective is critical for this assignment, given shareholder demands or my own CEO's or line executive's functional background?

Bennett was thinking beyond the norms of his job as a sales represen-tative. He had learned the value of brand promotion through powerful displays. He simply took the initiative to have a different impact.

One of our exemplars of "initiative beyond the call of duty" is Vineet, whom we wrote about in a *Harvard Business Review* article.[1] Vineet works in India for Swiss medical device company Synthes. The more-than-$3-billion company manufactures and markets implants and bioma-terials used in surgery and in the regeneration of the skeleton and soft tissues. Long before working at Synthes, Vineet intended to pursue a sci-ence career but also had a passion for improving the lives of people in emerging economies, such as his home country of India. This basic vision remained with him, but his career took an unexpected path.

After college, to the surprise of his peers, he chose accounting in order to gain financial expertise that would serve him well in any business career. He accepted a position with Indian professional services firm A.F. Fergu-son, which had a leading portfolio of audit clients. He then moved to Arthur Andersen (which merged with Ernst & Young) and eventually to KPMG in Gurgaon, India. But he increasingly felt that his work didn't match the priorities of learning and effecting large-scale positive change. So Vineet took a position at Synthes.

Early on at Synthes, he learned to always think like people at least one or more levels above him—the high-potential trademark that we've described. To achieve this perspective, Vineet had a habit of asking many questions—sometimes to the consternation of his peers and bosses—but he balanced his incessant questioning with an insatiable desire to deliver. Nobody could doubt his commitment to the work and the company, and Vineet's ambition was not a matter of personal triumph. As the country manager for India, he created a 150-page book celebrating the contributions of his colleagues and highlighting their common values. It became something of a textbook for the Indian operation at Synthes. It generated so much buzz that some employees who had left the company returned because the organization had been so energized by it and his leadership. No one asked him to write that book. No boss told him, "We need a celebration book." In other words, don't wait for your boss to guide you to the initiatives that could be game changers.

Vineet's original aspirations fueled his extraordinary level of initiative. To that end, he also produced an eighty-five-page business plan that included a vision for bringing world-class education to all Indian surgeons, including those in remote areas. Synthes's CEO has said that the plan changed how the company looked at India.

Vineet is deeply curious, but with a singular intent—to transform learning into actual initiatives. When he traveled to the United States for a Synthes strategy meeting, he stayed on for several extra days to be a "fly on the wall" with the US salespeople. Having gotten the CEO's attention with his growth strategy, he thought the company would be able to execute it only with the help of more and different employees. The US division appeared to have these employees in its sales force. Vineet went on dozens of sales calls, observing what made the sales force so effective. He then took what he'd learned to create a new sales-employee competency profile for India (along with changes in training and recruiting) that highlighted entrepreneurial behaviors, an attribute he thought crucial for delivering on the promise of the Indian market. His actions led to a significant increase in sales. No superior asked Vineet to study the US sales organization. It was his genuine quest to build a stronger organization that led to this personal initiative. All his peers had returned immediately home from New York after the Synthes strategy meeting, but Vineet had a bigger goal—to increase sales by learning from others' best practices and then applying them in a new approach.

Identify the ways in which you can show initiative beyond your job responsibilities, whether in raising standards, capturing opportunities that others have no time for, or solving problems that no one has yet addressed.

Take Stuff Off the Boss's Plate

Another area where you can truly differentiate yourself and prove your potential is to take on some of the work your boss does not like to do or is simply not good at. A question bosses always welcome is, "How can I help take some things off your plate?" It works even more effectively if you can identify a task that requires skills you've already mastered. This becomes a win-win. Your boss gets rid of it, and you look good doing something you know you do well. These activities are likely to be the core tasks we described earlier, except they are core tasks for your boss. By taking them on, you are allowing your boss to focus on signature tasks. So while others may not see this as making a significant impact (and others may not even be aware you did this work), it builds goodwill and cements trust in your relationship. Your boss may or may not thank you for it, but either way she will appreciate it. This is not a state of servitude to the boss but a genuine desire to tackle the challenges and opportunities facing your boss and the organization.

Jackie was offered a stretch assignment in the banking division of a global financial services organization—a promotion to vice president and regional operating officer in Germany, the bank's second-largest European operation.[2] She accepted it, even though the odds were against her. Nobody there had heard of her, and she knew little about banking. Her experience had been solely on the insurance side of the bank. The regional president had wanted someone with banking experience, so Jackie's biggest challenge was to gain credibility quickly. The German staff was accustomed to running its own show, so Jackie figured she'd fail if she couldn't get the team on her side.

Jackie resolved to make helping her new colleagues a priority. In her first three weeks, she met with dozens of managers and openly acknowledged that she faced a steep learning curve. She focused on achieving small wins on issues that had long been thorns in their sides but that no one had time to address. For example, she streamlined the process for opening new accounts. She aimed to take as much off her skeptical boss's plate as possible by asking, "What time-consuming tasks would you like to see addressed within my first ninety days—ones that you don't have time for or just don't enjoy?" She immediately worked on these. For instance, he disliked confrontation, an important skill gap for her boss. So Jackie tackled the issues that had great potential for conflict, such as redesigning planning processes and resolving decision rights. She gained a reputation with her boss as a problem solver and, as a result, her influence grew steadily.

The lesson here is to look for your boss's unpleasant tasks or skill gaps—ones that you can successfully tackle not just to make your boss's life easier but to make him successful too. You'll want to do this thoughtfully so you don't unintentionally call out his or her shortcomings. At the same time, ensure that you don't become overloaded yourself. We all have limits to how much work we can take on in a given day, week, or month. If you take on too many core (or other types of) tasks from your manager, you may find yourself unable to do your own work. If your signature tasks or core tasks were to fall by the wayside as a result, both outcomes could be disastrous. Unfortunately, nobody (not even your boss) will give you a pass because you were helping out. So figure out which tasks you should take on and where you need to draw the line.

Adapting to and Mirroring the Style Demands of Your Boss

Your performance in the four opportunity zones will potentially snag your high-potential designation. At the same time, you cannot neglect the stylistic demands of your boss. We have repeatedly seen high potentials lose their status despite outstanding performance—all due to clashes and misfits in style expectations.

As a subordinate, you need to find ways to be effective under the different work habits you'll encounter with your many bosses. Don't expect your boss to adapt to your style. Your current boss could be very collaborative. He may enjoy brainstorming with you and having energizing debates. Your next boss could be someone who does not like to brainstorm and will ask you to come up with a single option for every issue. Some will be data driven, schedule driven, process driven. Some will be strategic, and others will not. Some are morning people, and some are afternoon people. Some will approach work in ways so different from yours that you might even question their effectiveness—or yours. You'll have to bite your tongue and remind yourself that this situation is not permanent. Meanwhile, sense and adapt to your boss's stylistic demands.

Rene, a senior-level high potential, describes the differences between how she managed two CEOs that she reported to:

> They absorbed information in different ways . . . for example, Amy was looking for very little interaction. I always carefully mapped out my thirty minutes with her. I knew exactly what I needed to cover. I had a clear set of well-developed ideas. With Rob, my current CEO, it is more of a conversation: "Let's talk . . . don't come to me with big decisions, don't bring me lots of paper." With Rob, it is seven conversations to take a decision. With Amy, it was one conversation for the one decision. For another boss I had, she always wanted to know about me personally. I would take ten minutes of every meeting to accomplish the key decisions that I wanted to cover, and then we would talk about our lives for another twenty minutes. She knew the names of my kids, what school they went to, my husband's job.

Detecting the Ways You Need to Adapt to Your Boss

How do you accurately determine the style and behavior your boss is looking for? If you have a highly approachable boss, one effective way to conduct your detective work is to ask her out to coffee or lunch. Directly discuss her preferred work style. Whenever in doubt, ask in a safe and constructive way. Offer different work scenarios, such as how often you should meet, whether she prefers formal or informal meetings, and how she is going to measure your achievement of success in tangible terms. Ask her about the quantitative and qualitative measurements that will be marks of your success three months from now and at year-end. Then, if you feel brave enough, ask what success looks like two to three years from now as well. If you are lucky, the answer will be something like "Well, you'll be promoted by then."

In your first few months with new bosses, always watch and listen. Observe the topics they repeatedly discuss in meetings. Watch if certain metrics, goals, and priorities are especially meaningful to them. See which individuals engage them well and ask yourself what the boss finds so engaging about these individuals. Look at the boss's style of running meetings and the level of candor and pushback between the boss and the meeting participants. Look at his office. What does it tell you about his life, needs for organization, demands, and preference for scheduling versus spontaneous interactions? Notice whether the phone is often ringing or texts are coming in, which may tell you whether he is in the midst of something demanding or perhaps is simply well connected or a multitasker. Observe how and when he likes to communicate.

One high potential we interviewed mentioned that his boss was a big fan of texting. He shared that she could out-text his twelve-year-old daughter and often texted him after 9 p.m. He quickly realized she needed a great deal of updates and was happy to get them in text form. If your boss sends you articles, look at the topics, the broadness of the issues covered, what your boss wants you to do with the information, and what he wants you to think about more. Be very astute at listening and observing well.

Even small things matter, like attire. As one young high potential commented, "I will always wear a suit when I present to our CEO. I mirror her attire. I have never seen her dressed informally. My own manager is more informal. With him, I will go in with jeans." Another commented, "On my first day on the job with my new boss, I noticed how uncomfortable she became when a colleague offered up a statistic on a topic we were discussing. The boss asked in a questioning tone of voice, 'Where did you get that piece of data?' My colleague said, 'Oh, I remember hearing it from someone.' The boss's face changed into a frown. Right then, I knew that every time I offered up a point of view about a particular data point, I had to prove that I'd done my homework. I could not casually throw out statistics without backing up their source."

Pay particular attention to when your boss is most open to receiving advice, especially challenging information. Some bosses value feedback and debate, but not in front of twenty other people. Some expect you to tell them what's on your mind at any given moment. One executive told us that he knew that he could share sensitive information with his CEO on the company plane whenever the boss took off his shoes. At that moment, the boss was relaxed and ready to hear difficult feedback or discuss tough subjects.

Josh, a savvy high potential at a junior level, revealed how he starts off with a new boss in terms of situation sensing:

> In my first meetings with my bosses, my demeanor is fairly subservient. I will sit on my heels, accommodating. I will use that time to form an opinion about their style. My ability to read people is strong. I pay a lot of attention to their verbal and nonverbal cues . . . how they sit, how active are they in using their hands and facial gestures. I assess how successful they are at conveying a point, how important facts are to them, how opinionated they are about issues. For example, our CEO forms opinions quickly. It is extremely difficult to change her opinion. Once she has decided, her position becomes ironclad. So when I prepare content for her, I always work to stay on the right side of her perception by not directly challenging her opinions. For example, I had a meeting with her a day ago. I am setting up to propose a new product. I gave her the initial testing results from a customer experiment. In the end, she made a recommendation with which I did not agree. Instead of saying, "No, I think there's a better solution," to her, my positioning was much softer. I very deliberately chose to say, "We could do that," with my intonation suggesting there might be a better alternative.

Another approach to getting data about your boss is to ask current or former direct reports. Ask them what they particularly liked about working with your boss. What makes your boss successful—expertise, personality traits, or other skills? Ask them how your boss likes to work and run meetings, and what outcomes he expects. Sometimes you will get a straight answer, and other times, not, but the data is always worth collecting. Look out, however, for peers on the same team who might be highly competitive and attempting to mislead you. Given that there are only one or two high potentials for every ten peers, you are in a dead heat with the others, even though we'd like to assume positive intent.

With the most open and developmentally focused bosses, you can solicit real-time feedback after you work with them for a while. For example, we'd recommend getting feedback immediately after a meeting where you played a major role. Ask directly, "What did I do well in there? What can I improve upon next time?" You'll usually get concrete clues about what they want from you.

If you clash on a particularly important dimension of your boss's style, you'll see a negative reaction. You've most likely hit a style priority that is a *hot button*. These behaviors or priorities are *absolutes* for your boss. It might be that every meeting has to start precisely on time. Or only a one-page summary is needed on every issue you're assessing. For one boss, your relationships with company distributors might require your utmost attention. For another, it could be exceeding the safety targets. So it is imperative you determine the boss's hot buttons beforehand.

The bad news is that your boss will often not tell you the first time you trigger one of their hot buttons negatively. She'll hope it was unintentional on your part. But the second and third time you trigger that hot button, the boss will begin to doubt your capability. You'll then start to receive negative feedback or else notice that you are no longer given certain tasks or invited to specific meetings. You're in trouble by this point.

Most bosses have four or more style or priority hot buttons. They can be a minefield. A first step is simply to ask, "What would I need to do to really upset you? What are your absolute priorities in tasks, relationships, and style? What should I pay particular attention to? How do you like to receive data and information? What are your top criteria in making key decisions?"

How You'll Know You're in a Style Misfit Predicament

What are the early warning signs of a *style misfit* with bosses? As they lose trust in you, they will become more prescriptive. They will be constantly checking in with you to see how things are going. They'll want lots of

A CHECKLIST FOR READING YOUR BOSS'S STYLE

Use these questions to assess the range of stylistic choices you need to make and then match to your bosses' preferences:

- What types of information do they prefer for decisions and in what forms? How much detail do they want to see to make a decision and what types of quantitative and qualitative information? Do they want a single option or multiple options to consider? Do they want to consider unconventional options?

- What is their patience level or the speed at which they make decisions? Some want two hours to go through the analysis; others want a one-page report and ten minutes of conversation. Some want briefing materials to read days ahead; others do not.

- Are they comfortable with your intuitions or do they want to hear only well-documented facts and data?

- How do they like to interact with you and the rest of the team— spontaneously or with meetings planned in advance, one-on-ones or in a group, with the door closed or open, in your office or theirs? In person, on the phone, through FaceTime, and/or texting?

- How comfortable are they when you challenge their point of view? In what settings can you challenge them (e.g., one-on-ones)? Where or around what issues can you not challenge them?

- How far up the chain of command can you realistically take an issue? Do you need their permission at each step upward to discuss an issue with their superiors?

- How forthright can you be with them about your concerns or news about setbacks? Will they see this as a sign of strength or weakness on your part?

- How connected does the boss want you to be with them? "On call" at all times of the day and night or just during business hours? How often do you need to communicate during business trips or vacations?

- How quickly do they expect a response from a call, email, or text (immediately, within two hours, end of day, next morning)? What issues do they want to hear from you immediately?

- Do they want to be included only in certain communications ("Only copy me when I need to make a decision related to the communications; I trust you to handle the rest") or in all communications ("Always keep me in the loop, just so I know what's going on")?

- How much of your personal life and their personal life do they wish to share; in other words, are they private or public people?

- How do your bosses expect you to work with others? Do they want you to kick ass and deliver, no matter the ramifications? Or do they want you to respect relationships and bring an element of diplomacy and unity to the engagement of those who are implementing your initiatives?

- What is their perspective on workplace attitudes and attire? What quirky annoyances bother them that you should always avoid (e.g., never text in meetings, keep your sleeves rolled down, always wear a full suit and never tan pants or a brightly patterned skirt, never chew gum, no baseball caps in the office, no Birkenstocks or flip-flops at work ever, etc.).

- What are their career aspirations and motivators and how do they see their team members as part of these?

status updates. With regularity, they'll correct what you say or how you say it. They'll review your work before it goes on to their boss. A very bad sign is if they jump in constantly while you are presenting.

One boss explained how he now engages an individual who doesn't understand what the boss is expecting:

> I have one individual on my team who has not figured me out well . . . so now I provide them with highly detailed, prescriptive advice. For example, their current assignment demands say steps one through eight. In discussions with me, I realized that they did not see all of these steps. This person would have done it with only two steps and not understand the other six steps. So now I am watching how they do the next five. If they fall back to only those two steps again, I am going to be watching much more! Someone who is perceptive of my style will send me an email, "Hi Sven, Here are the seven steps I am going to undertake for this next initiative." So they will check in and be certain they are taking the right approach. This is what this individual needs to do.

Your responsibility is to adapt to the boss. Never assume it is their responsibility. Our checklist in the sidebar "A Checklist for Reading Your Boss's Style" provides the most important dimensions to consider when matching a boss's style and work preferences. Your task is therefore to figure out exactly how you need to adapt your style and priorities to your boss's.

Working with a Difficult Boss

Inevitably, you will have at least one bad boss in your career. A bad boss can be someone who isn't interested in you and your potential, doesn't care about identifying and promoting talent in general, is inept at managing, or simply doesn't like you. You just can't seem to impress her, or worse, you rub her the wrong way. If you are not careful, this boss can damage your standing. In the sidebar "Dealing with an Unethical Boss," we discuss what to do with a potentially more difficult situation—an unethical boss.

The key in these situations is to impress other stakeholders, particularly senior leaders. They will recognize your skills. Usually if you are a high performer, and you think your boss is bad, the good leaders in the company will already know your boss is bad. They will often understand you're in a tough situation, and at some point they will move you away from this boss. Handle bad bosses professionally and maturely. Remember that you are trying to impress other stakeholders who will watch how you handle a difficult situation. In some cases, if you can't escape from the bad or unethical boss, you may simply have to look for a new job outside your organization. Here are a few key lessons to keep in mind:

- Never assume that just because someone is your boss, he is always right. You owe him your point of view. With some, you'll need to be blunt in questioning decisions; with others, you might need to be more deferential and polite. Ask if he wants your input. If he says yes, offer it, even if he doesn't seem very grateful for it. If he says no, offer it anyway, but in the form of questions rather than statements.

- Use questions to ask your bosses what they think, how they feel, and whether they recognize the impact or effect of their decisions on other things or people. Difficult bosses usually respond better to being asked questions than they do to being told.

- Form alliances with other people who may be better at getting your boss to listen to certain things than you are. Use those relationships to test ideas and subtly deliver messages to your boss.

- Never compromise your integrity just to get a difficult boss to accept, like, or listen to you.

So how should you navigate these precarious bad-boss situations? The story of one high-potential leader, Quinn, illustrates how to approach this challenge. Quinn had just been promoted to be the director of operations within his business unit. He would be replacing a good friend who had

DEALING WITH AN UNETHICAL BOSS

You can go too far in adapting to certain bosses. You do not want to simply mirror your boss's style, becoming a Mini-Me like Dr. Evil's clone in the movie *Austin Powers*. Find what he or she wants to see in an outstanding direct report and adapt to that style of working as best and honestly as you can. You need to be careful here, too. If your manager is unethical or wants you to do something you feel is wrong, you need to draw the line. For example, he might ask you to do something that would undermine his boss or one of his peers so he can look good. You have to live with yourself at the end of each day. You have to guard the positive elements of your style and beliefs about the right ways to work and treat others. Simply being a sycophant and doing whatever he says (a "yes" man or woman) is not the answer.

One personality survey used for assessing high-potential status—the Hogan Development Survey (HDS)—even calls out this derailing behavior in a dimension called "Dutiful." It describes the behavior of individuals who are so eager to please that they become reluctant to act independently. They need the excessive advice and reassurance of their boss before acting. They

---

been demoted because of a poor relationship with Quinn's soon-to-be boss Natalie. She had a reputation as a very difficult supervisor. Before Quinn started the job, he called former subordinates of Natalie's who carefully advised him on how she liked to work with staff. He made a point of talking to individuals who were unsuccessful in working for Natalie and to those who had succeeded. From them, he learned approaches that worked and those that would make a poor impression on her. In his discussions, he discovered that her style was extremely different from his own. For example, Quinn, who is extroverted, loves informal and hallway conversations. On an impulse, he'll just pick up the phone and chat with someone about an issue. His new boss disliked this informal, spur-of-the-are also very reluctant to express disagreement with their bosses for fear of falling out of favor.

This takes situation sensing too far. These dutiful behaviors might work with the rare type of superior—the one who loves highly dependent subordinates. But in the vast majority of cases, your boss will value independent thinking and action. Without these qualities, you'll be seen as lacking initiative and depth. So don't ever sell yourself out to a boss. Don't compromise your core values or ethical standards.

When you get a boss who wants you to do something unethical or highly manipulative, hold your ground. You might ask, "I want to make sure that I fully understand what you are asking me to do. It feels you are asking me to do X, and I am frankly uncomfortable with it. Am I correctly understanding what you are asking of me and is that what you really want to do?" If you don't like the answer, tell your boss you have to decline the request because it goes against your principles.

Finally, above all, make sure you don't get caught up in anything illegal. Following your supervisor off a cliff while he makes bad decisions is not the right choice for anyone. This is why companies have confidential whistle-blower programs.

---

moment style. She believed it disrupted her well-planned days. So Quinn abandoned his informal style for the time being and planned every meeting with Natalie well in advance.

He also learned that she was a highly analytical boss who liked information always grounded in data. As Quinn explained, she was a "show me the numbers" person. She disliked brainstorming and intuitive approaches to decision making. So he made a point of briefing her on every issue, using quantitative analysis and data. He rarely brought her options to explore but instead data supporting a single option he felt was the optimal solution. Within a few weeks, Quinn's mirroring of Natalie's disposition on these few critical style dimensions had won her over.

But the real home run for Quinn in his relationship with Natalie was his discovery of a signature task that would have a high payoff for her. He knew that an ongoing priority for the operations group was its analytics—production data, cost information, safety performance. The department was not sophisticated in gathering this information or in communicating it. Quinn learned from some of his contacts that the top executives of the division complained that the data from Natalie's group was usually late and frequently inconsistent, taking between thirty and sixty days simply to close out the year's operations results. Getting better and faster analytics would be a highly visible win for both Natalie and him.

While it was not a task that Natalie had assigned to Quinn (or to anyone else), he sought her permission to work on an idea that would solve the issue. With a green light from Natalie, he went to work implementing a new technology that forced all the raw information through a very sophisticated dashboard. Within a few months, the technology was up and running, just in time for the year's close. That particular year's operations data was closed out and communicated in twenty-four hours. More importantly, it was accurate data compiled in meaningful categories, to the big surprise of the executive team. Quinn commented on the win: "We devised a system that was highly valued, highly accurate. I also accomplished it by not taking a lot of Natalie's time. In the end, it gave her and the department visibility all the way to the top."

Sometimes, however, it is simply impossible to resolve a conflict directly with your bosses. They may be difficult and seemingly inscrutable. In these circumstances, you need to put your head down, do your job to the best of your abilities (be sure to get the core tasks completed flawlessly), and focus on enhancing your network. Working with other leaders can help tremendously here. Even if you are not labeled a high potential under the current boss, having others aware of your capabilities will help you weather the storm until either you or your boss changes roles. For this reason, it is essential to have multiple sponsors to ensure you build a reputation beyond your boss among your boss's peers. Help them in situations where they can call upon you. Get involved in task forces and special projects to enhance your visibility within the organization. While your high-potential label matters, it most certainly can and will change with the next boss. Whatever happens, your performance history in an organization stays with you throughout a career given talent systems these days. A record of strong performance can help buoy you over the long term despite one bad boss's less than positive review.

One quality that many of our long-distance high potentials found helpful is the attitude that there is no boss you can't win over. You just have to understand why they act the way they do. All bosses want to be successful in some fashion. Your mission is to figure out how to help them succeed. The key question becomes whether you are personally comfortable in how they want help. One individual told us about a boss who was just downright disrespectful to his staff. He wanted results with no thank-you's and had no interest in motivating or developing his team. He was often rude and insensitive in daily interactions. Our high potential figured out how to win him over by basically driving himself and his team hard to meet his superior's unrealistic promises to a client. But once was enough. He told us that he wouldn't do it again because he didn't respect this boss and didn't want to manage that way himself. When he completed the boss's project, he requested a new assignment and a new boss. In the end, the old boss ended up getting fired for an ethics violation.

. . .

Situation sensing is the first of our high-potential X factors for a good reason. It is the foundational means for you to be adaptive, an important attribute of high potentials. You have to be able to read each of your bosses quickly and accurately in order to lay the groundwork for your success. If you support their success and help them to become high performers, it will reflect well on you in turn.

While your relationship with your boss is the most important, it's not the only one you must skillfully manage. In the next chapter, we'll look at other critical relationships in your journey to becoming a high-potential leader—your direct reports.

Summary Lessons

- Recognize that every boss you'll have is different.

- Learn all you can about delivering for your bosses both in terms of their agendas and the work habits they value.

- Focus your energies on the tasks that will help propel your boss's success.

- Tackle every assignment with the perspective that you're already at the level of your boss or boss's boss.

- Wherever you see an opportunity, demonstrate initiative beyond expectations to help solve an emerging organizational challenge.

- Differentiate yourself by doing the things your boss doesn't like to do. Be careful of becoming too much of a yes-man or -woman, though, and don't focus single-mindedly on achieving your goals at the expense of the organization and your relationships.

- Remember your responsibility is to adapt to the bosses; never assume it is their responsibility to adapt to you.

3

Talent Accelerating

How Focusing on Your Team's Development Multiplies Your Potential

Your boss designates you as high-potential talent, but it is your team that determines whether you can deliver the results to achieve that designation. You have to think carefully about who works for you, who you hire, fire, promote, and develop, and how. You have to be as interested in your team members' potential as your own. This is the core message of our second X factor, *talent accelerating*.

One of the most successful high potentials we've worked with, Eric, discovered this lesson painfully. In an early assignment, he had a mandate to turn around a product in serious decline. He devoted his first few months to undertaking an extensive listening tour of major clients, followed by a redesign of the product line and a revamping of the marketing strategy. Six months into the job, he sat down to review his results. At that moment, he realized the huge mistake he'd made:

> I finished at 90 percent of plan . . . which is really bad news in my company. I will never forget . . . I sat at my desk at 6:30 at night thinking this is crazy . . . Nothing is working. What happened?

I had completely overlooked the importance of my team's capabilities. I was so focused on learning from customers and product fixes that I had missed the fact that I had the wrong people in place. They were technically not up to the level to sell and service more sophisticated products. And not one of them wanted to be personally accountable for the changes we were trying to make. They were just biding their time until the next promotion.

It taught me a profound lesson—focus first on your team's capability . . . Only then can you get to the other stuff. In the end, I had to change out the entire leadership team . . . But I learned that the real job of a high-potential leader is to call out early on, "Who on my team can make the journey? Who cannot? Who can I develop? Who is a better fit somewhere else?" In every leadership assignment since that time—and I mean every one—I start out by assessing my people, the culture of the place, and then move on to the action plans, fixes, and performance goals.

Why You Might Not Fully Appreciate This X Factor

This absolutely critical insight—start every new role by assessing your people and culture—is paradoxically one that we see managers and executives fail to appreciate time and time again. You might ask why, given that it's so foundational to a high-potential designation. If you are like all aspiring high potentials, you arrived at your first designation because you were the best finance person or the best salesperson or the best engineer. You stood out because of your drive, mental horsepower, conscientiousness, and strong results. In other words, you personally made the difference. As you moved into early leadership roles, you were again the driver pushing your team to work hard, setting demanding milestones and goals, leading with a strong action orientation. You made sure to hit and then exceed your team's targets. If someone slipped up, you stepped in and sometimes even did the job yourself. As a result, you were the one who got promoted, not your team. Even our book's thesis—that a small group of leaders is uniquely talented—reinforces the notion that one individual makes the difference.

But here's the reality. This approach to what could be called "heroic leadership" is ineffective for long-term career success. As you gain seniority, it is no longer just about you and your competence. You are—and from now on will be—the product of a *talent multiplier effect*. The caliber and motivation of the individuals working for you profoundly determines your performance, multiplying it upward or downward. Fail to develop your reports' potential, and you will fail to develop your own. Imagine for a moment the consequences when the people working for you are underperforming leaders and think about the talent they are selecting, hiring, and promoting under them. It can't be good.

As we emphasized in chapter 1, mastering the skill of talent accelerating early in your career is critical. First, you'll have the time to experiment and learn, something you'll have far less of in senior roles. The risks to your credibility are a lot lower at the start of your career when learning setbacks have fewer, less visible consequences. Second, people are more likely to give you feedback and mentoring in the first half of your career. Third, you can catch your ineffective behaviors before they can become ingrained habits. So listen to and act upon what others have to say about your skills in spotting, developing, retaining, and leading talent. If you are not receiving feedback, be proactive and ask for it.

View Your Team as a Powerful Complement to Your Own Shortcomings

Obviously, your team is critical to your success. After all, you cannot possibly do all the work under your responsibility. You need lots of helping heads and hands. Effective high-potential leaders are masters at delegation and collaboration—knowing what to hand off and to whom and then how to hold everyone accountable for deliverables. But an even more important reason you need the multiplier effect of your team is that you are seriously incomplete.

What do we mean by *incomplete*? In our work with managers and executives, we have yet to find a well-rounded leader. They simply don't exist. Over our careers, we have been privy to tens of thousands of leadership assessments. The good news is that nobody gets a perfect score on all the boxes in their organization's leadership framework. Just like you, all high-potential leaders have important gaps in expertise, knowledge, and skills. In addition, most have habits that actually hinder their effectiveness. They also have responsibilities they don't enjoy and so procrastinate on them. When you're in junior roles, all these shortcomings are less apparent and far less likely to hurt your career. As you reach the middle levels of your organization, however, they can become career derailers.

No matter where you are in your career, your team is the most vital means you possess to address your gaps in skill, knowledge, and information. For every assignment, figure out where you need talent to complement you. For example, one high-potential leader whom we interviewed highlighted a disposition he needs on every team:

> My shortcoming is that I come across as leading from the head and not the heart. I am strong analytically, and so I communicate from this side. As I have led bigger teams, I learned, however, that you get a lot more people motivated through the heart. Connecting this way does not come naturally to me. I now pair myself up with the right human resources leader who helps me tremendously. They teach me what I need to demonstrate in a town hall meeting or else they remind me to send a personal note to someone. My initial awareness of this need for someone with emotional intelligence on my leadership team really all started ten years ago when I discovered that junior people found me intimidating. One of my direct reports at the time was really good with people. She pointed out my gap and coached me to be more balanced around the emotional side of leadership.

Be aware of what you are really good at (e.g., skills, knowledge, and capabilities) and what you are not. Start by thinking about the projects and efforts in the past when you were most successful and those where you underperformed (to your own expectations) or even failed. What about you and your skill set made the difference in these contrasting situations? Write these down. Thinking ahead, what skills, habits, knowledge, and tendencies (or dispositions) do you have today that you know will help you as your career progresses? What are your gaps in light of the demands of possible assignments over the next few years? Write these down as well. Now do a comparison and figure out what dispositions, skills, and perspectives you need to balance yourself. This is the list of complementary qualities you need to think about as you consider your team's talents. The better you know yourself—shortcomings and strengths—the better you'll be able to assemble and leverage a team of highly talented people.

How Does My Boss Assess My Capability at Talent Accelerating?

When your boss sits down to assess your talent accelerating capabilities, he looks at *how* you achieved your outstanding performance results, rather than simply *what* you achieved. This is very different from a traditional performance review where the emphasis is almost always on *what* you achieved. The sidebar "The Questions Your Boss Asks in Assessing Your Capability at Talent Accelerating" highlights the questions your boss will weigh when evaluating you.

If your organization's culture is highly relational, team-related dimensions often carry tremendous weight in your boss's eyes. Such cultures value the time you spend mentoring your reports, giving them exposure to senior leaders, and providing them with opportunities to develop. You are expected to actively invest in your best and brightest players, as well as address and resolve any situations with those who are underperforming. Bosses watch to see if you take or share credit with your team, hoping you do far more of the latter. They observe the level of trust you build with your direct reports. They weigh how safe your staff feels bringing difficult issues and especially bad news to your attention. They observe how you talk about your team members in public. Some organizations

THE QUESTIONS YOUR BOSS ASKS IN ASSESSING YOUR CAPABILITY AT TALENT ACCELERATING

- How well do you size up the talent of your individual team members? Do you have a good read on their strengths, areas for developments, potential derailers, and the ways in which they complement you?

- Do you build trusting relationships with your team members? Are they comfortable bringing you bad news? Can they share their ideas and solutions freely with you? Can they debate with you? Can they openly share their development needs?

- How well do you motivate your talent? Are they excited to work for you? Do you deploy a variety of means to motivate and do you tailor your approaches to the individual?

- Do you share credit and recognition for successes and achievements, privately and publicly?

- How well can you lead a team in terms of structuring effectively roles and responsibilities to leverage knowledge and strengths, addressing conflict, coordinating efforts, spelling out clear priorities and goals, rewarding, and holding individuals accountable?

- Can you identify and swap out a poor performer, and how quickly? Do you know which poor performers can be turned around through

even scrutinize employee engagement survey scores as an important indicator of your leadership potential. In certain cultures, failing to live out these talent-related dimensions of leadership can derail your high-potential status despite strong performance. We'll illustrate with the case of one outstanding young engineer who failed to appreciate the necessity of acquiring this talent-centric skill set.

coaching and role restructuring and which cannot? Are you effective in developing the former to become successful performers?

- Do you know how to invest in the more talented people, providing coaching, constructive feedback, assignments, special projects, and opportunities to present to senior leaders and work with important stakeholders?

- Are you an effective teacher and coach? Do your team members describe you as their mentor?

- Are you grooming successors for your own job?

- Can you lead people who have been your peers and friends, and hold them accountable?

- Do your team members look up to you as their leader?

- Do you avoid treating certain individuals preferentially, in other words, do you practice having no visible favorites?

- When assigning people to new projects, do you consider the strengths of the whole team and how each person can contribute?

- Do former team members want to work for you again or would they rather avoid you?

- Do you keep tabs on people that you have groomed in the past, and do you advocate for them even after they have gone on to work for other managers?

Dan was a brilliant but abrasive individual. He suffered no fools to an extreme. The content of his unfiltered, frequently curse-laden feedback to anyone who delivered less than outstanding results was the talk of cafeteria chatter. Given his high standards, he was extremely demanding and controlling. But he did deliver impressive results. With his performance track record, he was promoted to mid-management with this shortcoming intact. While each boss had counseled him to tackle his abrasive style, he could not see the value; after all, he was getting promoted. As he moved into middle management and now had teams of engineers reporting to him, the downsides of his style started to show up in more profound ways. While reviewing engagement scores across the engineering function, the head of engineering observed that whenever Dan inherited a team, the group's engagement scores dropped, and often significantly. Soon after a major promotion, two of his direct reports resigned, attributing their departure to Dan's insensitivities. The head of engineering decided he could no longer tolerate this lack of talent-centric leadership. Reflecting on the fact that Dan had never responded to the developmental feedback from earlier performance reviews, the boss decided that termination was the only solution. This promising engineer derailed because he lacked the X factors of talent accelerating and situation sensing.

How Do I Become a Talent Accelerator?

The critical question is: How do I cultivate the skill of talent accelerating? There are five core activities you'll want to master:

1. Calibrating the talent capacity of individual team members

2. Coaching and deploying assignments to test and harness each individual's potential

3. Tackling head-on the people who are not contributing to the performance of your team

4. Scouting out the best talent

5. Aligning your team's performance and behavior through your own commitment to personal development

The failure to be effective, particularly at this fifth dimension, has proven to reliably predict those who fail to hold on to their high-potential status. Let's explore each of the five.

Calibrating the Talent on Your Team

The people you manage represent a broad spectrum of talent, capability, and drive. When you step into your next job, you will inherit some individuals who appear to be highly capable and others whom you'll discover are underperformers. Rather than rely on someone else's assessment, your challenge (and some might say responsibility) is to get accurate insights into each person's capabilities, specifically, strengths and development needs. Learn about their career goals and motivations. Within a short time, you have to discern between those who are outstanding performers, those who are poorly matched for their roles but could otherwise become strong performers, and those who are simply less competent and should not be on your team. You also have to identify the areas where you don't have the talent to address rising challenges and opportunities. These talent gaps might be for existing work (e.g., perhaps a project is failing because the people on it are not capable) or for future work that requires a new type of skill set or expertise (e.g., unique knowledge in a certain type of technology that no one on the team has). After a comprehensive talent assessment, you can begin to identify whether you have the right folks to build an effective team. The process can realistically take several months.

Your first step is to look at a broad range of dimensions (functional skills, personality dimensions such as collaborative and networking orientation, strategic and analytical skills—for example, systems thinking—and leadership) that are the requirements for successfully achieving your team's objectives or the business strategy. Let's say you are a general manager, and the business goals for your region involve the successful commercialization of a new product line. You'd want to be sure you have the appropriate operations or supply chain, sales, and marketing individuals all in place (with experience having worked closely with R&D, HR, and finance). You'll need naturally collaborative people, due to the many handoffs required between functions to launch the new product line. You'll need a few individuals experienced in cross-functional leadership. If you are leading a team in marketing focused on developing a new campaign, you will want a mix of talented individuals with both creative and execution capabilities, that is, the idea people and the practical people. So it all depends on the business need and what you are trying to achieve.

Naturally, your direct reports' *current performance* should be at the top of the list of variables to consider. But we have observed too many executives and managers who place an overriding premium on this singular measure. To avoid just focusing on the latest performance ratings, it's more helpful to look at an average or blend of performance and results delivered over the past three years for each team member. You'll want to see if there is a consistent trend or a more mixed pattern. Look at their career trajectories to date. Draw upon as many different sources of information as your organization can provide, such as 360-degree feedback reports, past performance reviews, manager quality tools, or other tests or assessment grids that we will discuss in chapter 7.

The previous bosses of a subordinate can be a rich source of information, especially if they are very thoughtful about talent. Your peers may also have in-depth experiences with your direct reports from which to draw inferences as well. In addition, you may have a highly capable HR partner who knows your team members from prior jobs. Your observation skills are critical. Watch carefully how subordinates behave in meetings with you, your team, their direct reports, and senior leaders.

Of course, meet with each individual on your team. Ask about their career aspirations, find out what motivates them, and record (yes, literally write down) your observations. What do they want out of their careers? What is the next job they'd like to have? What critical challenges have they faced? What did they do in those situations and what did they learn and incorporate in their approaches going forward? What does each individual currently appear to be really good at? What are their gaps? In what situations do they tend to have a difficult time performing well? How are their relationship and interpersonal skills? Where do they need developmental help to become stronger performers? What kinds of assignments and coaching would be most helpful for them?

Take all this information and grade your talent using the simple framework described in the sidebar "Grading Your Talent: The A, B, Cs" within the first few months of your arrival into any new role.

GRADING YOUR TALENT: THE A, B, Cs

Whenever you step into a new assignment, use this simple method to sort your team into three groups: the highest-potential performers (A players), strong performers who consistently deliver results (B players), and subpar performers (C). While few companies actually use the labels A, B, and C (instead opting for terms such as high potentials, future leaders, continuity players, trusted professional, core player, growth employee, etc.), this three-category scheme is the easiest place to start.

Your A performers not only do their existing job well but also show great initiative and are capable of taking on far more responsibility. In essence, they are your high-potential talent. You want to accelerate their development and do everything you can to retain them. They most likely represent 10 to 15 percent of the individuals on your team.

Your B performers are strong contributors who make up the vast majority of your team and employees, in the range of 80 to 90 percent of the team. They do their job well and responsibly. As one interviewee mentioned to us, you can sleep soundly at night knowing these individuals are in charge of particular activities. That said, because they form such a large group, they show a wider range of initiative (from high to quite low), and some appear to have limited potential to step into bigger jobs (and as a consequence, some organizations break down this group further into various types of subcategories). Yet they possess the deep expertise or knowledge that you and your organization need.

Your C players are another story. You have to tackle their performance or behavior soon after stepping into your leadership role. We'll discuss what to do with C players later.

Once you have classified your talent into meaningful groups, you are ready to build a more focused talent management or staffing plan for your team. By using the classification scheme, you will be able to determine if, when, and where you need more As, fewer Cs, and how best to deploy or redeploy your Bs.

Developing Your Talent through Coaching and Deploying Assignments

Coaching skills are a baseline requirement for high-potential leaders. Hopefully you have learned these skills from several bosses who are outstanding coaches. But our experiences with managers and executives suggest that most are not sufficiently skilled at coaching. So you need to seek out training and opportunities to practice this skill daily.

In our research, we came across a talent-oriented boss who had honed a very effective approach to coaching that we consider a good model to employ. The boss would present to her direct report an actual issue she was facing as a case study, possibly a conflict between certain team members or a communications breakdown with another function. She would walk her report through the details and then ask what they would do. Afterward, she'd explain what she did in reality and what she learned from the experience.

With this approach, you are coaching your reports in your own thought process around the common problems they will encounter. Other examples of useful coaching practices include routinely debriefing with a direct report right after an important meeting—especially one involving top leaders. You could share your perceptions of what they did well in the meeting and its impact. If they were not effective, you would offer concrete suggestions for improvement and brainstorm how they can implement them.

Often, coaching can mean simply stepping back from what you are already skillful at and allowing your team members to develop that exact capacity. One high potential told us about her visit to a customer in Nashville with her sales team. She was explaining to the customer how her team would support the client. Midway through the conversation, she realized that her team of four individuals was simply sitting there silently as she spoke. She was doing what could have been their work. At that moment, she turned the rest of the discussion over to the team. They picked up where she stopped and went on to win more business from the client. So ask yourself, "What am I doing that my team members could do for their own development?"

One of the stronger differentiators of more skillful, talent-centered leaders is their tendency to coach in short bursts throughout the day rather than restrict themselves to formal coaching sessions. We often observed them providing feedback and insights to direct reports in sessions of a few minutes. The mindset that providing real-time feedback and coaching as a *daily* activity is critical to your success. If you see a team member doing something well, comment then and there. If, in contrast, they have room for improvement, find a time and place soon after that moment—and in private—to share your recommendations.

Max, a high-potential leader, shares how he does this with his most promising A player:

> I inherited an individual named Alex. People told me that he was sensational, but I didn't really know him. He is very driven. As a matter of fact, I was blown away by how proactive he is. But at the same time, he has a negative reputation for his candor. He tells you exactly how he sees something—no filtering. So the biggest thing that I have done for him is real-time feedback. He will get frustrated that someone is not cooperating and giving us the resource support we need. He'll come into my office and say, "I am just going to go see his senior executive about this person's lack of support." I will tell him that this approach is not going to work, that he can't handle the problem this way. I give him feedback right at that moment. We will brainstorm a more appropriate approach. So now when he finds himself frustrated and wanting to be direct, he swings by my office or calls me. We do a short debrief, and together we figure out the best way to address the issue.

What Max has done so successfully is to cultivate a developmental partnership with his subordinate. Alex knows his boss wants him to succeed, especially in his interpersonal skills. When he feels his frustrations turning into reactions that he might regret, he heads immediately to his best sounding board, Max. As a result, Alex is learning diplomacy, a critical skill if he wishes to secure and maintain his high-potential designation.

In addition to coaching, assignments are a critical element in your development toolbox. If you'd like to cultivate someone's leadership capacity, put them in charge of a task force. If you want them to learn to work with other functions, set them up as your department's liaison for a cross-functional project. If you want them to master presentation skills, have them do multiple internal presentations to your team. If you want them to cultivate executive presence, have them observe the executives you admire and then present to them. In all these cases, ask yourself and the individual what they need in coaching from you or others before they undertake the assignment. After all, they are stepping into these assignments requiring skills that they don't currently possess. Don't allow them to go into any of these situations unprepared.

Addressing Your C Players Head-On

Once you've determined whether you have any C players on your team, you need to manage these underperformers quickly. First diagnose why their performance is falling short. Underperforming C players most likely fall into one of three groups. They all deliver outcomes consistently below your expectations, but each for different reasons. The sidebar "Three Types of C Players" provides more details on each type of C player.

What to do about C players?

Do not procrastinate when addressing C players from any of the three groups; otherwise, their impact will cost *you* on several levels. First, your team will question your credibility. Running through their minds will be questions like these: Why does my boss tolerate this person's low standards or their terrible relationship skills or their micromanaging? Don't they see how demotivated I am working for this individual who steals credit or lacks initiative or interferes in my job? Why is this person blocking opportunities for people like me?

Every C player on your team fills a role and, in turn, blocks the advancement and development of your most talented people. In addition,

C players are rarely good role models or mentors. In its research on talent, McKinsey & Company found that 80 percent of respondents in a survey of several thousand executives said that working for a low-performing boss prevented them from learning, kept them from making greater contributions to the organization, and made them want to leave the company.[1]

What will get in your way when tackling these individuals' performance or behavior head-on? The primary reason will be emotional. In some cases, the C performer may be a former colleague or even friend of yours. In other cases, she is a long-tenured and loyal employee. Perhaps she is only a year and a half away from retirement. Maybe the individual is the former head of your department and even built it from scratch. For most of us, it is an emotional challenge to discipline or even fire someone we know or to whom we feel an obligation. The act is a painful one that we'd much rather postpone. You might also fear possible litigation or are simply annoyed by the onerous process of documenting their serious levels of underperformance. In the McKinsey research, only 19 percent of the thousands of senior managers it polled felt that their companies removed low performers quickly and effectively. We cannot think of any high-potential leaders who felt they moved too quickly on a C player. Most regret having given them too many opportunities and, in turn, too much time to prove themselves.

How can you identify your C players early on in your tenure as a boss? The most obvious signs of the poor performers are a lack of preparation for assignments, consistently missed deadlines, or a lack of serious follow-up on requests. They may accomplish only 40 to 50 percent of what you expected. They'll often blame others or external factors for their delays and incomplete assignments. They could even blame you for not giving them more precise instructions and expectations. You'll learn about your C players who lack interpersonal skills from colleagues who complain to you. When you see this pattern repeating itself beyond two or three incidents, you most likely have a problem individual on your team.

You need to hone your ability to fire poor performers. Don't put it off and don't make someone else do it for you. Get your boss's support, along with your HR contact and certain peers who might be working with

THREE TYPES OF C PLAYERS

Most of us associate the C-player label with someone who has been promoted beyond their abilities. They may lack real drive. They often hide under excuses for their shortcomings, blaming their peers, other functions, or external forces for their failure to meet performance goals. You have to test their competence by giving them assignments with concrete, measurable, and shorter-term outcomes. You have to be extremely clear about deadlines and metrics so you can accurately measure their progress. Ask them beforehand, "What resources and coaching do you need to achieve your goal?" Provide them with the realistic support they say they need. If they don't deliver, then you'll have a clear indicator that their competence and drive are insufficient. As Ray Bennett, Chief Global Officer at Marriott International, explains:

> It is critical to start with clear expectations. Make certain you convey concretely what good performance looks like—as well as poor performance. So they can understand the distinction. Let the person know the rewards but also the downside consequences for their performance outcomes. It's very important to provide training or coaching on how to accomplish the job duties. You may even have to retrain to reinforce the learnings across different contexts. I am also checking to see if there are personal circumstances that may be impacting their performance. Performance updates are essential at fixed time intervals making certain that each discussion is documented. If the individual is not meeting your performance standards after feedback, coaching, and documented performance conversations, then you have to make the tough call. In addition, it's important to show you don't give preferential treatment to your best people. Your poor performers can then claim favoritism. So I tackle this challenge by giving my best people

feedback on their areas for improvement in public so their colleagues can see that everyone on the team is treated consistently.

However, some C players underperform due to a serious mismatch between their responsibilities and their actual skills. Your challenge is to assess whether they have the capacity to learn the skills needed for their role or if they should move to roles that match more precisely their skill set. When you meet with them, ask what motivates them about their job, what things they would change if they could (and why), and what things they want to stay the same (and why). Another question that you can try, particularly if you are new to the team, is asking, if they were the boss, how they would restructure the team and in turn their own work. What role would they personally most like to have if they could? Where do they feel least competent? The answers may help you determine whether the circumstances have merely stifled them or if their performance is a true case of incompetence.

The other contributor to underperformance is a style clash with you as their boss. One leader we know was struggling with a subordinate whose formal and reserved style contrasted sharply with his own more informal and extroverted style. He wanted his subordinate to spend more time social-izing after hours with the company's clients instead of in formal meetings during the workday. In a moment of insight, the leader realized he had a rad-ically different conception of relationship selling than his subordinate did. He had never conveyed where and how he felt his direct report should spend time with clients. Once they talked and his direct report received some in-depth coaching, the performance problem resolved itself. Sometimes, you may need to step back as a boss and assess the ways in which you might be contributing to the performance problems of your direct report.

The C players in the third category achieve their results—often strong ones—but at the cost of relationships, both their teammates and cross-functional peers. They can be abusive, over-controlling, self-serving, or

(continued)

arrogant. They may demonstrate little or no interest in receiving coaching and mentoring. Many are drivers who enjoy muscling their way through assignments. They need very tangible feedback from you, linking their behavior directly to the negative consequences you are observing. You also have to be candid with them in terms of career consequences. Tell them up front what will happen if they continue with their behavior, even if it means alerting them to the fact their job or next promotion is at risk.

them. Be transparent in your assessments and honest in your approach with the poor performer. HR can help you if you are concerned or need to build those skills. You also must have a discussion with HR so that you have the right evidence for termination and the correct process. One of the great proof points of high potentials is their ability to do the toughest things courageously and to do them well and compassionately.

Do not try to move your C players to your peers' teams, especially if these individuals should not be with your organization at all. We call this "passing the problem," and it will result in serious damage to your reputation. Here is a cautionary tale about one high potential—someone we mentioned in our opening chapter.

A group of senior managers was assessed for their potential to be the future CEO of the company. The individual who scored the highest in the assessment process—the one who on paper had the greatest probability of being CEO—derailed his chances largely because of "passing the problem." He hired a subordinate who, on the surface, appeared to be a very high performer. Soon into the assignment, the individual turned out to be far less competent, or simply unable to adapt to his new role. The high-potential senior manager, however, was conflict averse. Rather than confront the subordinate and establish a performance plan, he told a peer that the individual was actually quite good. The senior manager even rated the underperforming person highly on a performance review because he couldn't deal with confrontation. He then persuaded his colleague to take this individual. Soon after the hiring, his peer realized that the new hire was indeed not competent. Word spread quickly about this "pass." The reality was that the senior manager was trying to be kindhearted and not ruin his subordinate's career. He also believed that this person would be a better fit somewhere else. Instead, the senior manager's peers interpreted his actions as devious. As a result, this high potential was quickly out of the running for the CEO job and was later pushed out of the organization. The message is that you should tackle your C players early on and provide them ongoing coaching and an opportunity to reverse their course. If they don't deliver by a specific time, let them go.

Scouting the Best Talent for Your Team

While you might think that finding new talent to replace those Cs—and even your Bs and As who are vacating positions—is easier to do than determining what type of talent you have on hand already, it is not. Whatever the state of the talent you find on your new team, you will almost always need to scout for new talent to increase the overall functioning of the group. The best place to start looking is internally.

Depending on the level of sophistication and size of your organization, this might range from informally talking about the open role to colleagues or in staff meetings to using a formal job-posting process online, where roles are listed (almost like "want ads"), and individuals post résumés and a matching system ensues.

The online job-posting (and often sourcing) system process can be useful. Implemented well, it can help in your search for different types of capabilities across your organization. In a small company, the online posting may not help, but it can be enormously valuable in a larger, global corporation. For example, imagine you need a programmer with capability in electromagnetic fields, yet no one in your local area seems to have that skill. You do a search online and find 150 potential hires with these skills scattered across the company. Selecting further, you screen for performance, language preferences, mobility, experience level, and interest. You send the five candidates who result from your screening the job request by email. Use the internal system judiciously, however, to ensure you are following the appropriate protocols for sourcing talent internally versus simply "stealing" the best people from other teams.

What if you cannot find the caliber of talent you need within your organization? Most internal job-posting systems have a simple policy. They will post internal candidates only for three to seven days, and then they automatically post externally on the organization's jobs website. So wait until after the internal posting period to find the external candidate you really need.

In some situations, you may find that there are strong internal high-potential candidates in other parts of your organization who you believe would do well on your team. They may have approached you in the past about wanting to work on your team. Either way, we offer a word of caution. If you are planning to recruit for your team using internal talent, it is best to work through your colleagues not around them—whether that is by using your organization's formal talent review process (see chapter 8) or simply by leveraging your internal networks. It is critical that you avoid "stealing" talent from other managers unless you want to create new enemies. Doing so will not only damage your reputation and status as a high potential, but it can also negatively impact perceptions of the person you have just recruited.

Being a Developmentally Oriented Leader for Your Team

The only real long-term path to high-potential status is to master the second X factor—talent accelerating—*by focusing most of your attention on your team's development and your own*. The following four actions cultivate this orientation.

1. Build development activities into your daily schedule. The high-potential exemplars in our research consistently carve time out of their insanely busy schedules to connect personally with the individuals they lead. One of the most impressive leaders we interviewed commented: "I really want the time working together with my team to be fun and engaging, and that is in the face of tremendously challenging work. I am convinced that strong relationships pay off. So I am continually investing in the 180 people in my group. I try to know as much as I can about how their work is going, and what their aspirations are and other aspects of their lives like their passions and hobbies. I find lots of small opportunities to coach and mentor them. I will freely share my insights about where the firm is headed or my experiences with a particularly important client."

Engaging your people through a concerted focus on their development is important. Ensure that each individual has a developmental plan, specific development experiences related to their unique needs, and ongoing coaching and feedback to develop skills and address critical gaps (and don't just rely on performance management reviews).

2. Make yourself vulnerable by encouraging a climate of constructive feedback and learning. Several of the most successful high potentials we interviewed spoke about the importance of being vulnerable as a powerful means to promote a developmental mindset in their teams. Arjun, a leader in a professional services firm, commented: "I usually have to reveal myself in some uncomfortable way . . . reveal that I have a problem and ask for advice . . . and trust the confidence that I can have with them. People want to see you, their leader, in a very human way. You have to be willing to allow yourself to be vulnerable. The payoff is that they become comfortable with being vulnerable, too, and in seeking feedback for themselves from you and others."

Research by two colleagues, Rob Goffee and Gareth Jones, reveals that when leaders share their weaknesses, they establish a deeper level of trust with their teams.[2] In contrast, managers who communicate that they're quite perfect, with no apparent weaknesses, are signaling that they need no help from anyone. They are literally the smartest person in the room. They can seemingly do it all. This is a deeply disempowering message to everyone who works for them and a great example of an *anti-talent-accelerated* mindset.

Revealing your shortcomings also invites a collaborative atmosphere and underscores your authenticity as a leader. But you have to be selectively vulnerable. Don't show too much to everyone or even a little to the wrong individuals. Don't reveal a shortcoming that could be interpreted as a fatal flaw—a flaw that suggests you are an incompetent professional. From the standpoint of talent development and engagement, the best option is to reveal gaps in your personal development areas where your team can help you. A young high potential in our study solicits feedback on his experiments with different presentation styles. Another is working on her coaching skills, another on delegation, and another on conflict resolution. In all these examples, they acknowledge their weaknesses and ask for ongoing feedback and guidance from their direct reports and bosses.

3. **Share your own development goals (and share the feedback you've received).** If you wish to be vulnerable in the most positive of ways, describe your own development objectives to your team members. Many of our high-potential leaders share their 360-degree feedback results with their team and then collaboratively choose one development area to focus their efforts on for the next six months to a year. Along the way, they solicit progress feedback from their team, checking in frequently to gauge their progress on their goal. This powerful modeling signals to your team that development should be everyone's priority, but that it starts with you as the leader.

4. **Remember that you sit in a spotlight.** As a high-potential leader, your actions and choices are under great scrutiny. The spotlight comes from all directions. Your reports put you there because you are directly responsible for their futures. Your peers are assessing whether you are their competitor or ally, a resource or a drain on their time. Senior leaders are watching to see if you will continue to measure up. Some endorsed you for the role, and your success or failure reflects directly on their ability as talent spotters. Perhaps you took the job they wanted for one of their own

high potentials who didn't make the cut and thus are watching to see if you fail.

That is a lot of people watching you. Tiny gestures, actions, and communications become amplified. If by nature you like to make faces or joke around, you now have to be careful. One high-potential leader said she had to stop teasing people because colleagues believed she was serious rather than joking.

You can, however, leverage this attention to signal your conviction in your team members and their development. One thoughtful, high potential said that he will not walk into a meeting room with his telephone but instead leaves it on his desk. He felt it was a sign of disrespect to be on his phone in the middle of a meeting with his direct reports or even have it in view. He also disciplines himself to ask four or five open-ended questions in every meeting before he starts to share his own views. He wants to signal that he genuinely values his team's opinions. He often changes the point of view he brought into the meeting after hearing their responses. He understands the power of his emotions and their potential to act as a contagion for his team. So he comes into every meeting conveying a positive energy.

The point here is that your daily, often small actions signal powerfully your interest in the development of your staff. So take the news of a failing project as an opportunity for reflection and exploration of the causes. Focus on next steps rather than simply expressing your anger and disappointment. When you are working on your own development area, alert your team, ask them what they'd expect to see you doing differently, tell them you'll be soliciting progress feedback from them, and then just do it.

. . .

The second X factor, talent accelerating, is what creates a multiplier effect for your own performance. The higher you go in the organization, the more that other people deliver your results, and the more you will need this multiplier effect to prove you are a high-potential leader.

How will you know when you have successfully mastered talent-centric leadership? Mark Alders, vice president of human resources at Avery Dennison, shared what we consider the true test—the difference in outcomes he sees with every true talent-accelerating leader:

> Let's say you have a fast-food restaurant chain with ten restaurants and with ten high-potential leaders running each of them. The true high potential is going to manage in a way where he or she can be absent for whatever reason, and the restaurant will run in the exact same way as if the leader were there in person. Basically, they spend their time building processes, teams, and capabilities, so it will run extremely well whether they are there or not. Over many years of visiting manufacturing sites, I have found the difference between high-potential leaders and average leaders presents itself very quickly. Many plant managers stay right by your side as you tour the plant and are uncomfortable letting you walk around by yourself, whereas the true high-potential leader will spend time with you and then step back and let you visit and investigate things on your own. If the plant manager who is not a high potential is absent, you will see and hear things they don't want you to see or hear, and things won't be running as smoothly. The do-everything-themselves "musclers" can run an operation up to the $100 million to $200 million range, but beyond that size, it becomes very difficult to muscle results. Such leaders are simply too controlling. They disempower their people, and they get overwhelmed.

So ask yourself, "If I were to leave my job today for a month, how would this place run without me? Have I done a great job of developing each and every one of my staff in ways that have allowed them to realize their potential? Have I built a team of complementary, talented individuals who enjoy working with one another? Did I create a strong bench of leaders who can do my job at a moment's notice?" A yes response to each will be the sign that you have mastered the critical X factor of talent accelerating.

Summary Lessons

- Your team will determine whether you are able to deliver the results you need to achieve high-potential status.

- All high-potential leaders have important gaps in expertise, knowledge, and skills, just as you do. Be aware of both what you are really good at (e.g., skills, knowledge, and capabilities) and what you are not. Build your team to complement your gaps.

- Master the five core activities we identified to be effective at talent accelerating.

- Continually engage your people through a concerted focus on their development.

- Convey in deeds that you are committed to development—your team's and your own.

- When it comes to assessing the talent of your individual team members, don't focus just on their current performance but their potential.

- Address your C players head-on and with a sense of urgency.

4

Career Piloting

How to Succeed at the Difficult Assignments Ahead

As you begin to demonstrate your leadership potential—and especially once you've been designated a high potential—you'll be promoted more rapidly than your peers and into assignments with greater impact and visibility. As a result, you'll be stepping into increasingly more complex assignments. They will be stimulating, profoundly rewarding, and nerve wracking. The good news is that you'll grow in ways you would never have expected. Most of these assignments, however, will be challenges so big that you'll sometimes feel completely over your head.

The *variety* and *scope* of jobs ahead will demand that you continually operate outside your comfort zone. By comfort zone, we mean *a reliance on the base of experience you have acquired to date.* At a certain point, you will find that you can no longer rely on your core expertise, say, finance or marketing, or your track record, say, the number of deals you've closed, or even on your leadership style, that fast-paced fire-fighter side of you.

To succeed in the surf ahead, you'll have to cultivate the third X factor, *career piloting*, your ability to quickly adapt to new situations by adjusting your mindset, flexing your leadership style, engaging your team and peers to solve and implement with a laser focus, and staying tightly connected to your boss. This X factor ensures that you will deliver on the high potential's promise of outstanding performance no matter how big or how bad your next assignment is.

If you'd like to gauge how you currently stack up in terms of career piloting, assess yourself using the questions in the sidebar "Are You an Effective Career Pilot?"

In this chapter, we will help you build the skills of career piloting. We'll show you how to:

- Become comfortable with a nonlinear career path that is both exhilarating and unpredictable, along with managing the risk associated with it

- Develop fundamental comfort with ambiguity and manage assignments that are fraught with uncertainty

- Work with your boss during challenging assignments and invest in your peer relationships

- Make sense of the different types of assignments and experiences you'll need to become a good career pilot

We'll also explain why some assignments might be bad for you and how to turn these down without sending the wrong message or damaging your future leadership potential.

Become Comfortable with a Herky-Jerky Career

Many of the opportunities coming your way will be way beyond your control. Wharton management professor Peter Cappelli and his colleagues Monika Hamori and Rocio Bonet looked at the career paths and qualifications of the top ten leaders in each of the *Fortune* 100 companies.[1] They discovered the relative lack of control that leaders in these large companies had over their careers. When compared with past decades, Cappelli and his colleagues noticed that "What we see now are more

ARE YOU AN EFFECTIVE CAREER PILOT?

- How comfortable are you going into a job where nothing is familiar? Do you approach every new assignment with an open mind? Are you inquisitive and versatile in your style? Do you thrive on new challenges? Are you willing neither to always have "the answers" at the start nor comfortably fall back on what you already can do well?

- Do you fully understand the agendas of your superiors as they relate to your current assignment? What's at stake for their careers? What outcomes would they consider as barometers of your successful performance in this role? How well have you identified and addressed their needs related to your assignment?

- Can you quickly create a culture of psychological trust with your team? In other words, can you create safe channels for information to flow to you, especially bad news and critical feedback? Are you good at explaining what's in it for them? Are you thoughtful about how you need to manage and what to communicate? Do you understand well the morale and engagement issues you face and how best to address them?

- Are you a calming influence on those around you in times of pressure, stress, and change? Are you able to foster an environment of open dialogue and entrepreneurial spirit when facing ambiguous situations?

- Do you know the peers you have to engage and win over to succeed at your new assignment? Are you clear on what you can offer them in return? Are you already winning over any naysayers?

- How maturely do you respond to setbacks? Do you pick yourself up and keep on learning and experimenting? When things go badly, do you blame others? Or do you accept responsibility? Do you learn from your failures and change your actions as a result? Do you possess a basically optimistic disposition—but not blindly optimistic?

'herky-jerky' careers. People stay in jobs during the recession a little lon-ger than usual, and then when they move, they don't necessarily move in predictable ways. They might leapfrog over others who have spent con-siderable time on the executive track; or people could be brought in from the outside and put ahead of lifers whose own career track then becomes more questionable, perhaps causing them to move as well."[2]

In other words, you can't predict the assignments you'll be given with any certainty. You have to be open to what is offered, even if it's not what you originally wanted to do, and take a long view of your career. You'll be in a better place for success if you focus on what you can learn from your upcoming, unexpected assignment, whatever it might be, instead of the promotion you were dreaming of.

Ping—a division president—describes the evolution of his high-potential career:

> I started out managing a function in our finance organization where I was responsible for everything just below the director's job. The director job opened up when my boss was retiring, and I had my heart set on it. I was super-qualified, along with several candi-dates. To my real surprise, I didn't get the promotion. I was told that if I really wanted to be promoted to the director level, I would need to move to another part of the business. I remember thinking that I was in a job that I really liked, and by every indication I was doing really well. The director's role seemed like my natural next step. When I was passed over for it, I was thinking to myself that I was at the end of the road in my career. In reality, though I didn't appreciate it at the time, that role was several steps above mine.
>
> Several months later, I got a call from an internal client who approached me with another job offer. It was a real stretch assign-ment, a completely new area for me. I had to be effective working through other people rather than supervising. I was also younger than everybody else, so I asked myself, "How can you influence others who have so much more experience and expertise?" I took it and became the manager of field operations managing all the field construction. I did that job for two years.

Then one day a company officer called to see if I wanted to be the head of the emergency operations area. I said, "Should I have interest in that job?" My boss told me that it was good to be open-minded about the offer. I interviewed and was ultimately hired into that job. It too was a big stretch assignment. My job was to prepare for a range of emergency scenarios. In my final interview for the job, I felt like I was in a Senate confirmation hearing. I even had to interview with the CEO.

After that role came a real surprise assignment. My earlier boss—who had passed me over for the director job I had really wanted—called and said she had a job for me in external affairs that would provide me with a strong external focus. I took it and learned more in that one year than any other year of my career. Now I was interfacing with different external constituencies, some friendly and some not. My entire career up to that moment had been internally focused.

Then a year later, I was moved into the director job that I had aspired to some years earlier. Who would have guessed? I took all these other assignments not knowing that I would ever come back to that job.

As you can see from Ping's career, you'll have far more variety than high potentials of some twenty years ago. That earlier generation moved in lockstep through a function—assistant product manager to associate product manager to product manager and so on. That's not likely to be your career path. In the past, organizations were much more stable, so it was easier to plan concrete, structured career paths. With the world changing so rapidly in terms of technology, globalization, and digitization, it's not as easy to know what's next. Organizations change their structures and roles all the time. One company we know prepares employees for this phenomenon by saying, "Don't aspire to a specific job ahead of you as it might not be there by the time you are ready for it. Instead focus on what roles you can learn the most from next. A career is a lattice, not a ladder."

Don't have rigid expectations about a neat and tidy building-block career. In one of our interviews, we learned of a promising high-potential candidate who was turned down for the designation because he told his boss the exact three assignments he was expecting. His lack of flexibility waved a red flag that he didn't possess the mindset needed to be a long-term high potential. Often, someone is thinking carefully about your next step, but not in the linear manner you are. So be open to assignments even if they seem off track to you. If you are truly a high potential, your organization is probably planning for your long-term career destinations in the talent review process rather than simply the next promotion (for more information on how talent reviews work, see chapter 8).

The lesson here is to actually build as much variety into your career as possible while paying critical attention to the foundational experiences that your organization expects of its senior leaders. You literally want a "herky-jerky" career. High potentials who go up a single functional ladder their entire careers are far more likely to tap out than you.

The High-Wire Challenge of Promotions Ahead

Along with the unique and varied opportunity stream afforded to high potentials comes an intensifying spotlight. Top managers are now paying an inordinate amount of attention to your performance and particularly to the ways in which you achieve it. They are watching to determine whether you have the right stuff to become a senior leader. If you consistently perform at or above expectations, you will continue in this virtuous cycle of promotions and special opportunities. At the same time, the risk to your career is growing much higher. Your failure to master the essentials of career piloting in a singular assignment could derail your high-potential status.

For example, an executive shared with us how his direct report lost high-potential status based on one particular project, which revealed a critical shortcoming in his skill set and a corresponding lack of responsiveness to address it:

> Given his track record to date, I thought Mike would continue
> to be a high-potential performer. He's good at creative thinking,
> at proposing strategic ideas to reinvent our business models. He
> also has great subject-matter expertise and is really strong at

partnerships and networking. But I discovered that his big gap is on the execution side, getting things over the finish line. He cannot meet deadlines. That's a serious shortcoming since we are under intense scrutiny by our top executives to meet hard-stop deadlines. It's actually now the most important part of his job.

For instance, I put him in charge of leading a big strategy engagement project. It took him longer than a year to complete it. Something he should have accomplished in six months. While he is very strategic, I learned that his other shortcoming is translating his insights into clear ideas and communicating them well. His presentations are more a collection of random ideas. It is far less than what I was expecting from someone who sees things from a strategic view.

I have given him honest feedback about both of these shortcomings and have coached him. But I have to say that he has not been open to my feedback. He thinks that he has it all covered, that he does not need to improve. So at the start, he looked like an A player, but I now see him as a B player.

The point in this example is that demanding assignments up ahead will reveal your gaps—often dramatically—whether you want them to or not. Your gaps will become acutely apparent to your bosses. This level of visibility of both your strengths and shortcomings is the price of entry into every high-potential designation.

Be open to feedback that may painfully zero in on a personal gap and be highly responsive in taking corrective actions. You cannot rest on your track record of past promotions or believe that your other strengths will make up for a shortcoming. If your boss sees deadlines as targets that cannot be missed, you have to deliver, no matter how highly you think of the other strengths for which you were promoted.

Let's look at the mindset you'll need to safely navigate the surprising career twists and turns of high-potential leaders. It requires a fundamental comfort with ambiguity, a quality you can develop. It's foundational to the X factor of career piloting.

Getting Comfortable with Ambiguity

To become skillful at piloting in turbulence, you have to cultivate a fundamental comfort with opportunities beyond your control and often far outside your experience and knowledge. We call this a tolerance for ambiguity, a quality you can develop over time. It entails a high tolerance for situations that are increasingly undefined and unpredictable. It requires that you be at ease in reaching out and engaging your most pivotal stakeholders to help you cultivate a keen understanding of the landscape ahead and to coach you in the skills and knowledge soon to be demanded. You have to cultivate a broad and versatile repertoire of change-agent skills. You must also be prepared to be flexible in your style and actions and be strongly oriented to learning and, more often, relearning.

That said, it's easy to lose this openness. Your success at achieving a high-potential designation can and will easily foster a misplaced sense of confidence. After all, each promotion tells you how talented you are. You now have a track record of performance that feels like an insurance policy protecting you against future setbacks. As well, your self-confidence has been an ally in achieving high-potential status. Your confidence will be one of the reasons why you accept this next assignment without serious reservations. If you didn't have that confidence, you'd likely turn down the majority of the opportunities coming your way, acutely sensing how truly difficult and demanding they will be.

We want you to shake off some of this confidence and stay a bit paranoid. Why? In our research and consulting, we have seen high potentials derail in their middle and later careers because of overconfidence. It led them *not* to focus on their developmental needs related to a particular assignment. It led them to underestimating the homework and resources needed to succeed in that next demanding assignment. When things turned bad, their acceptance and comfort with the growing ambiguity disappeared.

Always assume that each new role ahead will demand that you flex your style and build new sources of expertise and skills to succeed. Keep reminding yourself that no one really knows the true extent of your potential in every new assignment until you've actually proven yourself. After all, you've never done your next job. Your superiors may even have overestimated your versatility and ability to learn or perhaps they don't fully appreciate the power of a particular shortcoming or expertise gap to derail you. They may not even appreciate the impossible requirements of the assignment they've just given you.

Guard this touch of paranoia. If you do, you'll be far more likely to undertake the extensive homework required to accurately assess and pilot the next highly challenging assignment. We offer additional lessons in the sidebar "How to Manage Ambiguity in Your Assignments."

Now we turn from the mindset needed to succeed at career piloting to the relationship you should never overlook or underappreciate when you enter each assignment designed to truly test your potential.

Leading Your Boss As You Pilot

When Harvard Business School professor Jack Gabarro looked at managers stepping into new and challenging assignments, he discovered that the single most important difference between successful and failed assignments was the new manager's relationship with key stakeholders by the end of their first year.[5] Those who ended up with failures had poor working relationships with their bosses. A conflict in style around the issues of control and delegation was the most common reason. They had failed to clarify expectations up front for each other's beliefs about what effective leadership for the assignment entailed.

Given our discussion of situation sensing in chapter 2, we know this finding will not surprise you. Superiors are your most important relationship for your high-potential status. You have to ensure clarity and agreement on a broad range of expectations with your boss. For example, what exactly is your mandate for this assignment? How will your team's overall success be measured beyond the traditional core metrics of your organization (sales, costs, productivity, etc.)? Who are the critical relationships

HOW TO MANAGE AMBIGUITY IN YOUR ASSIGNMENTS

- What worked so well in your last assignment—with regard to process and knowledge—may not work so well in the upcoming assignment. Harvard Business School research shows that your strongest tendency in a new assignment is to make changes in the areas where you have the greatest experience.[3] So you have to cultivate breadth in your attention—strong investigative skills that look beyond your expertise and your experiences to date. Ask yourself: What do I really need to learn here—and from whom? What aspects of my style do I need to revisit and reinvent to succeed in my new situation? How will my prior experience and functional background potentially blindside me in this assignment? Where might I fail to pay enough attention because I don't have sufficient experience and perspective? What new relationships must I build, even if my time is limited?

- You are likely to be under tremendous deadline pressure, so your learning curve has to be steep. You have to leverage everyone who has deep insights into the context surrounding your role and implement these insights quickly. One absolute requirement is that you should spend time learning *before* you take the new job by leveraging your network of relationships to provide you with a rich, composite picture of your real priorities up ahead and the pitfalls you may face.

- You will likely be stepping into situations where you may not have long-standing relationships and where politics may be rife. Your experience base and networks in these new environments could be of limited value. Seek out former mentors and peers who know the politics of the place, who can warn you about the land mines, and who can guide you on navigating them.

- As you reach the middle and upper levels in your organization, your stakeholders are multiplying in different ways. More will be peers who don't have to help you or who simply have many demands on their time. You may actually find that some are your competitors. One of them may even have lost the race to get the job you just won. Suddenly your networking and relationship-building skills become paramount, but they may be skills that you've never taken too seriously until now. On top of that, your time is more precious yet investing in relationship building becomes essential.

- You need to have a clear sense of how you behave under pressure. Think about which of your derailers are likely to be triggered and how you need to mitigate them in stressful situations. You will be under great scrutiny not just from bosses but also your own team. Former vice chairman of Goldman Sachs Robert Kaplan observed that if you shield yourself from blame or avoid admitting mistakes or take credit for accomplishments rather than sharing, you are giving license to your team members to do the same.[4] He noted that if they fear your reactions to bad news, you will discourage the flow of candid and urgent information. Ask yourself: Do I lose my temper under pressure or remain calm? Do I protect my reports when things are not going according to plan or do I blame them? Do I accept responsibility for missteps? Do I publicly criticize my team or an individual when an outcome goes badly or do I do it in private? When under pressure, do I advocate what I feel the real issue is to my superiors? The right answer to each of these is clear. Your job is to practice these appropriate reactions with great consistency.

from their perspective, especially with peers and the boss's superiors, that you need to handle with care? How does your boss want to be updated and involved in decisions?

Michael Watkins's research on a leader's first ninety days in a job is particularly helpful.[6] He identifies five critical conversations to have with your boss as you step into a new role. We've summarized and added to Watkins's original questions.

The first conversation is about how your boss sees the *situation* you are stepping into, which ties directly back to our first X factor—situation sensing. You'll want to discuss the boss's perceptions regarding the following: What factors make this assignment challenging? More precisely, what are the early obstacles you'll face? What history has powerful implications for what you need to pay attention to? Who will be your natural allies? What is the caliber of the talent you will be leading? Where are the early wins? What are the agendas of senior leaders for this assignment? What's urgent to address or achieve? How much cooperation or conflict exists among the key groups and stakeholders?

The next conversation is about *performance expectations*. What does your boss need you to accomplish in the short and medium terms? What tangible outcomes do superiors want? What constitutes success, in concrete terms? How and when will your performance be measured? What are the absolute priorities to tackle? What would be alternative, acceptable outcomes if setbacks occur or pivots are needed?

The third conversation is around *style*—back to the message in chapter 2. How much independence can you have in accomplishing this assignment? On what issues and decisions should you seek guidance from the boss and with what frequency? How does your boss prefer to communicate? How often and in what forms—in person, in writing, on the phone, through texts and emails? How do your styles differ and where will you need to adapt yours to theirs? What style does your boss consider most appropriate for this particular assignment? Does your boss always expect you to be on top of certain critical details? How comfortable is your boss with you taking an issue up the chain of command? Or does the boss prefer to be the gateway to information to superiors?

The next critical conversation topic is *resources*. Define resources broadly. Yes, you may need funding or more people, but sometimes you need "air cover" from a boss or you need her to call on her networks for political support or other resources or the participation of peers. So, across the range of resources, what do you need to succeed and how can you secure it? What do you need specifically from your boss? Can you lobby superiors or even peers?

The final conversation is about your *personal development*. What does your boss see in this role for your own development? How will it contribute to the developmental goals you have been working on or want to work on? Are there courses you could take to build your capabilities for this assignment? Are there individuals who can provide coaching and mentoring around specific demands associated with the job? Can team members complement your own gaps in style, expertise, or knowledge?

As Watkins notes, the five conversations don't need to occur all at once. Your early conversations will likely be around diagnosing the situation, expectations, and style. As you progress in the relationship with your new boss, you'll be better positioned to negotiate resources, revisit your initial diagnosis of the situation, and in turn, reset performance expectations. When you feel you have established a comfortable relationship, you can raise the personal development conversation.

Now we turn to the individuals who will ultimately ensure you succeed in your career piloting efforts.

Engaging Your Team and Peers

We further know from research on new managers that those who fail in their assignments often have poor working relationships with their team members and peers. These groups of stakeholders become more pivotal to your success for two reasons. First, as you move beyond your functional base, you can no longer rely on your expertise. For example, if you are moved laterally into HR, you can't become an overnight expert in compensation or performance management. So you need complementary experts. In essence, your dependence on your team becomes greater.

Second, your most complex assignments will almost always involve other functions. Your peers have to actively support and implement your initiatives. Not surprisingly, Gabarro discovered that "taking charge" failures also occurred when the manager's relationships with these two groups of stakeholders were characterized by rivalries, disagreements over goals, conflicts in styles, and differing beliefs about what constituted effective performance.[7] The underlying common problem was the manager's inability to establish shared expectations to which all parties could agree.

Similarly, in his research on successful career transitions, Watkins observed that leadership at its core is about leverage.[8] To attain that leverage, you have to mobilize the commitment, energy, and actions of your team, superiors, and peers. You may stand on their shoulders, but only if they choose to allow you. New leaders also commonly fail whenever their early actions alienate the peers they need to be potential supporters. Contrast this with the case of Joel Albarella, who oversees his company's portfolio of innovative technology alliances and capital investments. Early on in the role, he learned this critical lesson:

> Most corporate venture groups don't end well. They tend to be misaligned with the incentives of the core business or are the pet project of a senior executive who turns over. As a result, their initiatives don't embed in the organization.
>
> Our own challenge is exploring new business models. I have had to build the right trusted network internally to test these models. To gain acceptance, I tell my team that this initiative is not about us, but the group business that is testing and putting the resources behind a new model. If we want our group and the technology to be sustainable, it cannot be about us. We may come in with the concept, but the unit knows the business. The key is being deferential with credit. We cannot order them to test a new technology. We cannot brag about what we did for a particular business unit. My original team wanted to get the credit for sourcing new technologies. I explained that we have to be smart about what

the business needs are and then ensure that the business leader succeeds and gets credit for this. The credit has to go to the business leader, not us.

In conclusion, build a strong network of cooperative relationships at the start of each assignment. Think about peers, boss's bosses, and subordinates' subordinates. Find ways to help them with information, favors, resources, political support, and so on. Keep your schedule flexible in those early days so you have time to develop critical relationships.

Make Sense of Different Piloting Assignments

To be effective at career piloting is to figure out how to successfully navigate in a new world, every time. The learning goals of *depth*, *breadth*, and *stretch* will shape the types of assignments you'll encounter ahead.

Your early-career assignments usually build *depth*. They deepen your functional expertise so that you are professionally competent in a domain like finance, marketing, information technology, or human resources. You need sufficient depth in a specific area (sometimes called a hip-pocket skill) so that you can call upon those skills whenever you need them.

At some point, you'll be moved into rounding-out roles either within your function or across functions. These, of course, cultivate your *breadth* of perspective. Some organizations, regardless of which function you grew up in, expect that you will have learned the foundations of all major business functions by the time you reach the most senior levels. PepsiCo, for example, as part of its people planning process, ensures that senior leaders have a solid proficiency level in a variety of functional domains including financial sophistication, deep customer and consumer knowledge in the industry, and an understanding of the business innovation process.

Next, you could be given a turnaround or a new venture assignment that will teach you the importance of versatility in your leadership skills and help you acquire new bases of knowledge. These *stretch* assignments push you to learn outside your prior experiences. If you have yet to get a

THE ASSIGNMENTS YOU'LL ENCOUNTER AS A HIGH POTENTIAL

Deep functional dives tend to come early in your career. Their aim is straightforward. You have an opportunity to cultivate your depth and breadth of expertise in finance, marketing, sales, operations, and so on. Here you demonstrate your professional competence through outstanding performance in your starting function.

Rounding-out or broadening experiences are opportunities to cultivate your expertise, breadth of perspective, and network of relationships. These often begin in early career with horizontal moves within a function, say, in supply chain services where you might go from contracts to financial settlements. The idea is to expose you to how all the links in supply chain services interact with one another. Later assignments will broaden your experience across functions, for example, a move from finance to human resources or from an internal operational role to a customer-facing role.

The test here is to see if you can be influential in building a broader network of cross-functional relationships and to deepen your enterprise perspective while delivering on outcomes that have real value. You may also be assessed on your ability to find common ground between the needs of the business units and the corporate center.

From there, you may step up to become president of an operating division. You are now dealing with multiple markets, customers, and even countries. You report directly to the corporate center where you will continue to deepen your enterprise knowledge. You now have the opportunity to address any knowledge and skill shortcomings that you may have for an executive role, for example, understanding the drivers and key assumptions behind corporate reporting.

External constituencies roles are assignments that place you in direct relationships with major customers, Wall Street analysts, professional organizations, regulatory or political bodies, activists, and even major consumers—all the external forces that shape an organization's ultimate performance. These are critical rounding-out assignments filling in gaps in your enterprise perspective. Promotions to these roles can be a promising sign that you are being groomed for high-level roles in the enterprise.

Turnaround assignments test your operating leadership skills on a variety of fronts. Here you have to make structural and role changes and/or painful downsizing decisions, and address demoralized employees. You will learn crisis management skills and the importance of establishing the right priorities. If the turnaround is within your function, it is a deepening experience. If the turnaround involves multiple functions, it is broadening and far more challenging. Because your predecessor most likely failed, the assignments are high stretch and high risk. You too may fail. The organization you have just inherited is tense and afraid. The good news is that you will usually have more latitude in acting. You'll also face less rivalry from subordinates who were bypassed for the assignment.

Big transformational roles are those in which you have to demonstrate strong change-agent skills. These internal infrastructure projects cut across divisions and business units. They disrupt the status quo and often face serious resistance. You need to engage and lobby powerful constituencies within the organization and to work across most, if not all, functions. This will test your communications, influence, networking, and change-agent skills. These roles are among the greatest stretch assignments, the highest risk to your career, and often the ultimate test of your career piloting skills.

Startups or joint ventures are the assignments where you build something from the ground up, such as a new organizational unit or capability. These assignments cultivate your marketplace, strategic perspective, and entrepreneurial skills. You will quickly realize whether you are comfortable with ambiguity. At the same time, these roles can be lots of fun, given their lack of structure and positioning in emerging growth opportunities—the product of different industries intersecting in new and exciting ways or emerging technologies or new marketplaces. Often, however, they sit outside the core of the business. As a result, your organization can be low priority and your visibility can be lower. The core businesses may even see you and your organization as a future threat. Keep your enterprise leaders constantly engaged in and supportive of the venture. You will learn the importance of bosses providing air cover. To succeed, you'll need to cultivate strong internal selling and championing skills and strong and constructive networking skills. These are stretch and breadth assignments.

Headquarters roles can vary widely depending on the structure and roles of your corporate center. In a centralized model, corporate might have a broad range of functional roles (e.g., all of R&D, IT, operations, marketing, sales, and HR); in a narrow model, corporate is primarily a finance or treasury function. So a high-potential assignment in the latter would primarily be as a senior finance officer. These assignments matter primarily at the vice presidential level. Below that, the roles tend to be more administrative and distant from the real action. But if you end up assigned as a vice president at corporate, you'll be expected to learn systems thinking and have a global mindset, navigation of senior executive politics, collaboration skills from working across business units, corporate functions, global markets, and external communications and statesmanship.

market-facing assignment, you soon will. The aim will be to deepen your marketplace and strategic perspective. Again, the goal here is to cultivate *breadth*—externally. In some functions such as finance, this might take the form of doing a stint in investor relations or communications, while in sales, it might mean relocating to live and work in the same town as your most important customer or supplier.

From there, you will likely be assigned to a bigger turnaround or a transformational project that cuts across functions and perhaps divisions. This tests your capacity to see the enterprise as complementary functions that have to be aligned. Called "systems thinking," this is an important capability for senior leaders to cultivate if they are running large, complex organizations. These breadth-building assignments are also a chance to assess whether you can influence your peers from other functional areas. So now you are experiencing both *stretch* and *breadth* internally at the same time. All these career moves broaden your knowledge, extend the range of your leadership skills, and test your potential through complex initiatives characterized by crisis or opportunity.

Many organizations categorize high-potential assignments by market type (e.g., domestic or global, country or continent, mature or emerging); product categories; business units; functional, or cross-functional, or headquarters; growth or turnaround situations. Some of these assignments are what we call *entry requirements* to the executive suite.

Look carefully at the backgrounds of recent entrants to the executive level. For example, do you need to spend time in a chief-of-staff role, a global assignment, or a headquarters role to count toward your C-suite requirements? But be careful about using current C-suite leaders as the only guidepost for your focus. As we've stated, the paths that today's leaders have taken may be quite different from what lies ahead for you. Moreover, as organizations have become savvier about building breadth through experiences, you might find new requirements that leaders never had to deal with themselves. The sidebar "The Assignments You'll Encounter as a High Potential" highlights the different types of assignments and the potential learning outcomes associated with them.

When Should You Say No to an Assignment?

Although you can learn something from every new assignment, not all are equally valuable in your career. Some will almost certainly derail your career unless you have a firm commitment from your sponsors that you will be able to move on even if you are unsuccessful. You may wish to turn these assignments down, if you can. They essentially set you up for failure unless you possess superhuman capabilities. These assignments fall into four categories:

1. The business or function is steeply declining, with little chance of recovery

2. The project is steeped in political jockeying between warring factions where only one side will emerge a winner (or none will emerge until the entire senior leadership power structure changes)

3. The project is at the edge of your organization's future and threatens the core business in profound ways

4. The job entails working with a highly dysfunctional boss

In all four categories, the risk of failure is very high, and as a result, you will likely lose your high-potential status. How do you turn down these opportunities in ways that don't send the wrong message? You need to do some skillful planning and communicating.

First, be sure you have all the facts about the prior incumbents or context that might set you up for failure. Then have a discussion with the individuals who have a really good grasp of the situation you'll be stepping into, from multiple perspectives. See if your homework matches their conclusions. The last thing you want to do is sidestep an opportunity because you misread the scene.

Second, based on discussions with your boss, HR, and others about your goals and aspirations, see if the goals you have articulated align to the role offered. Does this role help you obtain the critical experiences you need? While it might offer unique learning experiences, might you acquire them elsewhere or at more opportune moments in your career?

Third, if you are deep in ongoing work in your current role and don't have a successor ready to take over, suggest that it might not be the best time for you to leave your current post. Your decision makers might see through this excuse, but it is worth a shot.

Next, use your network of relationships (your boss's boss, the head of the function, or a senior HR executive) to convey your concerns and see if there are alternative assignments. Sometimes only your boss or one senior player is recommending the dangerous role for you. If you can work your own political skills in the background, you may be able to get more senior leaders to intervene without you even having to turn down the new assignment. This jockeying takes strong relationships and communication skills, but it is also exactly what any high potential might do.

Fifth, tackle the issue head-on with your boss and others. If you can present a strong case for why the role in question has consistently derailed others, you might be able to negotiate a "return ticket" or "get out of jail free card." If you are really persuasive, your boss might agree and find a different assignment for you.

For example, Ken, a superstar performer, is a known high potential in his organization. He had turned around a major brand that had been struggling with a new marketing campaign; he had since rotated through several different developmental assignments. He was gaining both depth in marketing skills and breadth across several business units. His career path was clearly headed toward senior general management roles. Given that, he needed his next assignment to round out his functional perspective. Ideally, he needed experience in a totally different function, such as operations, sales, or even running a small business unit. During his talent review process, however, a key role opened up as the chief of staff to a senior executive in finance. On paper, this would be a strong development fit for him. Ken had never worked in finance, and this would on the surface seem like a good (but not ideal) next role. At the same time, Ken had heard whispers about the poor success rate of those who had held the role before; three of the last four incumbents entered as high potentials but left as average players. The word on the street was that the senior finance leader was extremely challenging to work with and that any time spent with him often resulted in a derailed career.

When Ken was offered the role, he evaluated the situation and sought the advice of his mentors. They felt that while the experience would help him in the long term, it would only build his capability in finance. Another assignment outside of a staff job like this might be more of what he needed to continue his accelerated development, if he were willing to wait for a different opportunity. As a result of his discussions and a compelling argument for needing field experience next (not another staff role), he sidestepped the finance job without having to turn it down officially. In the end, it was offered to another high potential. Ken went on instead to take a joint venture assignment that needed staffing. The individual who took the finance role, however, was not so lucky. Nine months later, after mismanaging his relationship with the finance executive, the person left the organization entirely. Ken continued on as a high-potential leader.

. . .

Career piloting requires that you carefully evaluate every situation you're about to step into, thinking broadly and deeply about the context, requirements of you and your team, stakeholders, and resources. To master this skill, you have to continually learn, seek feedback, clarify the critical priorities, measure progress, experiment, and demonstrate versatility in your leadership.

Next we look at the skill that, like career piloting, becomes more important the higher you go in your organization. It's the fourth X factor—complexity translating.

Summary Lessons

- Expect to have an unpredictable career path with a tremendous amount of variety.

- Cultivate a tolerance for ambiguity—a fundamental comfort with opportunities beyond your control and often far outside your experience and knowledge.

- As you enter the stream of high-potential talent, an intensifying spot-light will be on you. Upper management is now paying an inordinate amount of attention to your performance and particularly to the ways in which you achieve performance.

- Because of their complexity and visibility to senior leaders, your high-potential assignments are far more likely to reveal your gaps, shortcomings, and bad habits. You have to be highly responsive to developmental feedback and act upon it quickly and successfully.

- Remember that what worked so well in your last assignment—with regard to process, knowledge, and style—might not work so well in upcoming assignments. You have to ask yourself: What do I really need to learn and from whom? How will my prior experience and functional background potentially blindside me in this assignment? Where might I fail to pay enough attention because I don't have suffi-cient experience?

- While almost every assignment is designed to help you grow, you may be offered one or two that you should decline. Be thoughtful about how you turn down these opportunities.

5

Complexity Translating

How to Turn Data into Compelling Insights

One common misconception about high potentials is that superior intelligence wins the day. On this score, we have particularly good news for you. Being the smartest person in the room is not an advantage. We have actually seen it become a roadblock for high-potential candidates, who can be perceived as arrogant, overly imposing, or just plain impractical.

There are, however, particular smarts you do need to develop—our fourth X factor, *complexity translating* or the ability to synthesize seemingly disparate data and information into strategic and relevant insights, and to communicate those insights in a way that advances the organization. Your high-potential status doesn't rely on being the smartest person in the room, but on connecting the dots and helping others see those connections.

This skill becomes more important the higher up you go. And the lack of this skill is why some people stall out and never make it to a higher level. As you advance, you will be expected to take information of all kinds (problems, goals, data, trends, ideas, alternatives, scenarios, outcomes) and distill them to their most relevant components. You'll be rewarded for

WHAT'S EXPECTED OF AN EFFECTIVE COMPLEXITY TRANSLATOR

When you are masterful at translating complexity, you'll understand what those at each level of your organization—direct reports, superiors, or peers—need to know so that you can tailor the content of critical information to each stakeholder in highly meaningful and actionable ways.

Your direct reports are looking for clarity out of the many priorities you have for them. They want to know clearly the absolute priorities that should command their greatest attention. They want to know what your signature tasks are and how they can contribute to their achievement. In addition, they want to feel your positive energy and motivation to help them achieve these outcomes. They want to know you have confidence in them.

Peers are generally more interested in your team's specific goals and objectives that directly intersect with theirs and how they will directly benefit from partnering with you and your team. You'll need to spell out clear lines of ownership, calling out the boundaries between projects, and making sure accountability expectations are understood (e.g., what's in versus out of scope for your work and your peers? who owns what?). Where different peers and their teams have significant interdependencies, you'll have to explain how you will work together effectively and not create redundant

clear, critical insights that help your colleagues solve vexing problems. If you're skillful, you'll be able to deliver meaningful and actionable insights in every possible format—a presentation to your peers that lays out a compelling strategic plan, a kickoff speech when you inspire your team to implement a new vision, a simple and focused discussion with your CEO about a certain new initiative that needs a major capital investment. You will be recognized for your ability to make the right translation for each level of the organization you are influencing (see the sidebar "What's Expected of an Effective Complexity Translator"). In the case of one of work. Above all, however, they will be looking to see what you can offer them (and what you want from them in return).

Your bosses, in contrast, are most concerned with whether you have the right priorities and have identified your resource needs, key milestones, and potential barriers, and plans to address them. They also want to see whether you fully appreciate how your plans affect their agendas and those of their superiors. You'll want to demonstrate your ability to think through problems they ask you to solve, articulate a compelling solution, and scope out detailed implementation steps.

Finally, senior executives will expect clear, thorough thinking about the impact of your work on the enterprise's agendas. In addition, they expect you to exhibit a style and tone that reflect a senior perspective. When presenting to senior executives, you should know that the focus of their attention can vary. While they are evaluating your content, they are also considering other elements about you simultaneously, such as your executive presence, your responses to challenging questions, and the overall caliber of your thinking and enterprise perspective. They will test you for other types of capabilities that are not explicitly part of your presentations or communications with them, just to see what type of leader you might be. Be ready for any one of these meetings to take an interesting turn to other topics, despite your planned agenda.

---

our high potentials, a presentation to the top one hundred leaders of his organization on a complex strategic decision dramatically accelerated perceptions of his talent and led to a string of advancement opportunities.

Some bright individuals who are successful in junior roles advance to senior-level positions, only to be stopped dead in their tracks because they cannot succinctly communicate their insights. Sometimes they get lost in the data itself, a trap called "analysis paralysis." Other times, they unintentionally overwhelm their audiences with their rigorous analysis. With either outcome, their insights are lost in a far too complicated translation.

We open this chapter with a real-life example illustrating the powerful difference that complexity translating made in a high-potential designation. From there, we explore the skills that underlie this X factor and how you can develop them. We'll provide guidance in how to read and respond to your audiences at a moment's notice, especially when you get an unexpected or probing question from a senior leader who is testing your skill at complexity translating.

Complexity Translating Skills
Make the Difference

Recently, we were part of a leadership program in a large organization aimed at developing the next generation of junior executives. The individuals who were participating in the program showed early signs of the potential to assume senior roles. While traditional classroom experiences were aimed at improving the participants' skills and knowledge, the real test of the participants' potential was the action-learning portion of the program. Although participants might not have recognized it at the time, the project (a business case to solve) and the resulting presentation to senior leadership were critical in designating them as high potentials. Projects like this, which are typical in accelerated leadership development programs, are something to watch for when you are invited to participate in one. Never take a presentation to senior leadership lightly, even in a team setting, or one based on a case scenario, however real or fictitious.

For the action-learning portion of the program, the participants divided into two teams. Both groups had the same business case to solve. Each team had to craft a new business model for an emerging product line of electric automobiles. The task involved collecting competitive data, analyzing consumer preferences, and determining the best possible manufacturing and go-to-market strategy, given certain organizational constraints. Both groups had a fixed block of twenty minutes to present their case and recommendations. Their audience included executives from the various heads of major business units, a few selected functional senior vice presidents, and the head of HR.

Each team could choose to present however and whatever it wanted. Although there was no right answer, only one team's ideas would be endorsed for implementation. So there was a healthy sense of competition. Each team member had a portion of the presentation; individuals were evaluated for their clarity of thought, how well they connected the dots between the different presentations of their team members, and their persuasive point of view. Our X factor of complexity translating would be on full public view.

Both groups engaged key stakeholders, gathered extensive data, and worked collaboratively to build their story. When presenting their findings, however, the two teams took very different approaches. The group called the Vypers went first. In an effort to demonstrate their deep understanding of the data they collected, the team developed a fifty-six-page presentation detailing their findings and solutions. It included an opening section on the history of the automobile and early trends and failures in electric technology, followed by consumer preferences for different options, new designs for the future, pending legislation that could either enable or derail the effort, alternative design solutions if the primary production model failed, and even samples of the marketing campaign to roll out the Vyper electric model.

The presentation was thorough. If taught in a classroom setting or perhaps as the briefing for a major internal program campaign, it would have worked well. Unfortunately, when Bennett (the first presenter) opened with the history lesson, several executives immediately began to challenge the information. The session quickly devolved into a debate over facts. Rather than adjust her approach based on the devolving situation, Mira, the next presenter, went deep, as planned, into the data on consumer trends. The conversation with the executives continued to veer once more. This time, they questioned whether the team had used the right types of data-collection methods. Ten minutes later, their time was up. The two remaining members didn't even get a chance to present. In the end, the team was unable to convey the Vyper design to the executive committee, let alone share the go-to-market plan.

They had lost all their work in an overly detailed, ill-paced, and rigid effort. While the foundational data collection and insights were superb, the translation did not align to the demanding requirements of the senior executive audience. In the end, the executives did not think that Bennett, Mira, and the rest of their team had delivered an effective solution. Their status as high potentials collectively was put in question.

Next, the team named Renew presented its case. This group had undertaken similarly detailed data gathering, but decided upon a different approach. The members crafted a streamlined ten-page presentation with a singular and reoccurring message regarding their solution of a renewable energy platform using solar technology. Each presenter had five minutes to cover just a few slides. They had designed the recommendations to capture the same key elements as the Vypers (e.g., consumer insights, production challenges, regulatory environment, marketing plan) but used a far more concise, well-aligned, and highly compelling narrative.

David, Amy, and the rest of the Renew team each breezed through their pages and key messages, finishing their presentation in the allotted time. Their theme of renewal was reiterated throughout. They used the data they had collected sparingly but in ways that demonstrated their command of the essential consumer insights, without getting lost. They showed simple graphics to drive home key points. They used text in punchy, lean ways for maximum impact. They had all the backup information nearby in case they needed it.

When they finished presenting, the senior executive review committee expressed positive impressions of the Renew team's presentation and recommended that its solution be carried forward. The Renew team members were confirmed as talented individuals with the potential to become more senior leaders by demonstrating their ability at complexity translating. This capacity was the singular difference between the two teams.

You might wonder if this type of process is fair. After all, judging an entire team's potential status based on a single collective presentation with only a few minutes allotted to each person seems extreme. What if you were on a similar team whose members were all duds, except for you? If you had been on the Vyper team, could you have salvaged your part of the presentation?

Unfortunately, just as a single breakfast or lunch meeting with a hiring manager can at times determine your selection for a leadership role, so can a single presentation propel or stall your career trajectory. Teams are a fact of life in large organizations, particularly when solving complex problems (e.g., task forces, short-term assignments, new leadership teams in a turnaround situation). As the success of the team goes, so goes the success of its members.

Although your hard work as an individual contributor is judged early in your career, team outcomes start to weigh more heavily as you progress up the organization. Senior leaders assume that if the team members are unable to work well collaboratively and produce a compelling perspective, then they must not have collective cognitive capacity. Whether or not you are directly responsible for the overall caliber of a team presentation, it will still reflect on *your potential*.

You might try to rescue yourself from a bad outcome by quietly blaming your teammates. We see high potentials make this basic mistake later in their careers, trying to distance themselves from teammates when the ship is sinking. It conveys to everyone that your character is questionable and that your leadership skills are lacking.

What Does It Take to Be Effective at Complexity Translating?

How do you learn to translate complexity, derive new strategic insight, and communicate that insight effectively to all your different stakeholders? The skills fall into three straightforward steps: (1) scanning for data, (2) integrating for insights, and (3) synthesizing for storytelling. You can use these steps when approaching almost any business problem, project, or presentation. They are generally sequential, though they can be iterative at times (e.g., some insights might lead you to ask new questions and seek new data to answer them). Consider how effective you are and where you need to hone your skills. We will explain how to develop each one and avoid the traps in each.

Scanning for Data

Obtaining relevant data includes identifying both readily available information and new information. The average manager, for example, will gather what's at hand and draw upon experiences to date. As a high-potential leader, however, you have to go beyond this all too efficient approach to bring a much broader perspective to the issue.

For example, if your boss asks you to explore how best to build a culture of innovation within your organization, you'd reach out to involve R&D (what are we innovating today?), HR (how are we training for innovation and rewarding people when they innovate?), IT (what systems and technology do we have that support innovation sharing and networking for ideas internally?), and sales (are customers actually purchasing our innovations or what types of innovations are they willing to pay for?). You'd look at examples from parallel organizations as well and examine the failure stories along with the successes. In contrast, if you collect information and data too narrowly, say, only within your own function or only what's at hand, you won't show that you have a strategic view.

Being a high potential also implies a passion for learning (more on this in the next chapter). It means demonstrating that you are open to knowledge beyond your current job, function, or even organization. This is why the concept of building knowledge in other disciplines outside your core function—particularly as you progress to more senior leadership roles—is so important. For example, start by reading broadly beyond your normal business or trade magazines. If you're in operations, get a subscription to *Advertising Age* and the *Economist* so you can see what's happening on that side of the business and in your overall industry. If you're in finance, catch up on the latest industry developments in technology or R&D. Read up on the powerful trends and factors in your regulatory environment. Think about how these might have implications for your own work and function.

Sam, an executive who started his career in the operations function, has a master's degree in engineering, but has a voracious appetite for staying current in other areas of the business, including finance, technology, and information systems. As a result, Sam suddenly found himself in a new role driving the design of an IT platform integrating data systems across the operations' function. Because the project had a strong cost-savings component, the finance and IT knowledge he gained on his own, coupled with his formal engineering background, made him a perfect choice for the new role. Three years later, after a successful run at implementing this new platform, Sam was again tapped for a different experience, this time in human resources. Today he is a senior vice president leading a major transformation of a global HR systems optimization effort. He has already started exploring the use of robotics (another area he has been reading about) to enhance service delivery times for highly repetitive call-center work. Sam would never have guessed that his broad interests would shape his career so directly. By being able to integrate data and insights across different disciplines, however, he has become invaluable to his organization and is on track for even bigger and more strategic roles.

Practices to develop this skill. High-potential leaders know which questions to ask, where to look for data not otherwise immediately available, and how to leverage their networks to obtain the information they need. So the next time you are presented with a new problem or situation (however large or small), consider the importance of scanning more broadly by asking yourself these simple questions:

- Beyond the information and data I have available, what's missing that I need to gather at a fundamental level? If I were looking at this issue from the perspective of each of my organization's different functions, what information would I want to know? If I were looking at this issue from my CEO's and my superiors' perspective, what information would I want to know?

- What other factors might play a role in affecting the project or objective that I am working on? In what ways will these concretely impact the processes, the people, the organization, or the external environment in which the situation is unfolding?

- Do I have sufficient depth of information on each topic area? If not, do I know what I need and where to go get it?

- What else am I not considering but should? Who should I engage to help me understand this situation from different perspectives? Who is the most expert on these types of issues? Who would have novel ways of thinking about this?

Pitfalls. There are several pitfalls to watch out for. First, you still need to deliver on your agenda and produce strong results. You're only a high potential as long as you are performing. Spending too much time scanning can distract you from getting results. Find the right balance. Additional pitfalls include the following:

- **Thinking you know more than you really do.** When in the data-scanning mode, it is perfectly acceptable to ask for information outside your knowledge base. That's the point. If you think you know something but you are wrong, it will come back to bite you later. So do your homework with rigor.

- **Relying too heavily on others to do your thinking for you.** Although you can't know everything yourself (this is particularly true in team settings such as the earlier action-learning example), be sure you and others are clear about which elements or issues you own and are driving forward yourself. If the initiative involves a team, be sure to influence the team's direction as much as possible so that all of you come out ahead, but don't do everything either.

- **Sticking too close to what you already know.** Beware of thinking "I've seen this movie before." An important factor in the context, business environment, or people dynamics may be different, and therefore the outcomes may not be the same this time. Use your experience wisely but don't use it as an excuse not to do the due diligence work.

- **Going too broadly and deeply into areas that may be irrelevant in the end.** You need to balance breadth and depth of data collection with speed and relevance. Those who go too deep are seen as narrow and limited because of an overreliance on their expertise, and those who go too wide are seen as superficial in their analysis. Think of the concept of "sampling." Get enough information to help you understand and go deep where it may influence your thinking or where you know your senior stakeholders are interested. But, in general, scope out the work and the data efforts wisely to the appropriate scale of your project. Ask well-informed colleagues and superiors if you are in doubt about gauging the ideal scope.

Integrating for Insights

Once you have all the data you need, move to the second step in the process—integration. Strong complexity-translator skills involve pulling data together in a framework, analyzing it using appropriate methods (e.g., statistical techniques, thematic approaches, financial modeling, Big Data analytics, etc.), and then converting that collection into something holistic and integrated. In short, you need to turn data into insights that ultimately influence actions.

More than just summarizing information in tables and charts, or using descriptive statistics or creating narratives, you need to make sense of disparate information, or "connect the dots." This critically important skill cannot be underrated. Just because you have all the right data doesn't mean you know what to do with it or how the pieces fit together.

At this stage, you are either creating new hypotheses or testing existing ones (or doing both at the same time). You are looking for more than just facts and relationships to result from this process. *You want to generate insights that will lead to actionable decisions* for the business. This is harder than it seems. Differences in the sources, quality, and timeliness of the information all play a role in how you should treat, analyze, and weight the data into insights for decision making.

For example, suppose you are interested in increasing the sales of a key product. The question you have from a business perspective is which levers will have the most impact. While you have many options at your disposal, they are not all equal in cost or complexity to implement. So you need to make choices using data-based insights. When you ask for input from various functions, you find out that marketing has consumer insights data indicating that engaging a new spokesperson (e.g., the latest teen idol singer) will drive greater brand awareness and, hence, sales. The operations team, however, has data indicating that the plants are at maximum capacity already, given the current setup. By adding another production line to each of your four major plants (coming from an operations framework), you can increase capacity by 25 percent, thus meeting the need for increased sales. R&D has a different answer entirely. Its consumer taste research indicates that hazelnut will soon be the new hot ingredient, and a product extension that includes hazelnut extract is required to boost sales (remember the framework is focused on innovation). As you consider these options and connect the dots, you decide to invest in the additional production lines in the short term and drive the R&D agenda for the long haul, while asking marketing to tie the new teen idol to the innovation when it's ready. Case solved, right? Not exactly.

Two years later, after spending millions of dollars on equipment, marketing, and R&D, sales have not improved; in fact, they are declining further. What's going on? Unfortunately, even though all the data from each group was accurate and important, it turns out not to have been at the root of the challenge.

The issue of declining sales was right in front of you, with your sales employees and their incentive system for selling more products. Your company had modified its salary structure to limit bonuses as rewards for exceeding sales targets. While this had seemed like a smart cost savings at the time, the declining sales data was never connected to this change because it resided within the HR compensation group and not with line management. In short, while the data (and the lever) was right in front of you, everyone else had their own compelling data and insights. This made it difficult to identify the right path forward, even though you connected the dots you had at the time. Finding the real root of the problem would have required an even broader perspective and generating additional insights that, in hindsight, mattered.

The last thing you want are data-based insights that miss the boat entirely, or statistically significant findings created from data that has no real meaning for the business or results in a bad decision leading to a decline in profits or performance. You have to ensure that you make all the right connections in a highly integrated fashion before you can zero in on a solution.

A test of your complexity-translating capacity. Your ability as a "data hound" ensures that your team and other stakeholders understand and make the right connections in the information you've collected. Your ability to be a complexity translator determines which data is analyzed and how, whether you are working in a small team or running a large organization. The data is there. You are the key agent who ensures it is evaluated in the right way. Senior leaders look for this early high-potential sign when they are working with junior talent. For example, when superiors ask you the following questions, they are testing your complexity-translating capacity:

- I like your findings. Tell more about how you got there and what sources you drew upon? What, if anything, surprised you? Did you take a novel perspective on any of the issues you identified?

- You shared the following facts . . . These particular ones did not have data to support them. Do you have data or is none available?

- What other relationships did you test for or consider? Why did you choose not share these?

- What hypotheses (or assumptions/thoughts) or key questions did you start out with? Where did you end up? What led you to abandon certain ones?

- Can you walk me through your thinking on this? What assumptions are you making? What are your sources for these assumptions? Are any of your assumptions based on intuitions?

- How did you get from X to Y? What were you thinking? What made you ask those questions? What were the catalysts for changing your original perspective or solution?

- Did you ever consider XYZ? Why or why not?

- What if I told you I had my own data that counters your findings?

At more senior levels, your capacity to answer these types of questions in a sophisticated manner will shape perceptions of your strategic-thinking smarts. In the end, getting this step right takes a combination of technical skill (in data management and analysis), intellectual horsepower (in thematic integration and analysis), and street smarts (in determining a key actionable insight for the business). We'd also advise you to role play with a trusted colleague asking similar questions to the ones above before every important presentation. We offer further suggestions for honing your skills in these areas in the sidebar "Skills That Increase Your Value as an Insight Integrator."

Pitfalls. Some pitfalls to watch out for are:

- **Making spurious connections among data.** Altering data to say what you want it to say or to create a more compelling story is unethical and can lead the company to make decisions that will harm it and potentially get you fired or worse.

- **Choosing the wrong people (or missing some key ones) for input.** This can send unintended signals and create resistance to your projects before they have even started.

- **Sharing too much information.** In some contexts, sharing too much information with others can be dangerous, for example, for competitive advantage reasons (externally) or political reasons (internally). Don't accidentally tell others what is going on in the company (e.g., a pending merger) when that information is confidential. Don't surprise your boss with information that she is not supposed to have (e.g., a more senior leader has asked you to take a new job to run a project that your boss might have wanted for herself). Be aware of what your manager might think if certain information, data, or decisions got back to him or her in the wrong way or at the wrong time. In some cases, you might tell them what you have heard about a pending organizational change or a new product launch, but recognize the potential risks.

- **Getting lost in continual searches for more information.** Eventually, that next level of detail or new data run won't add much. It will not only slow you down, but will create perceptions that you are inde-cisive or unable to meet deadlines.

- **Networking too much with others to continually gain information or perspectives.** Similar to analysis paralysis, "stakeholder paral-ysis" is the issue here. At some point, you need to end the iterative process and move forward. People who take too long to create connections are written off as indecisive.

Synthesizing for Storytelling

The final step in being a complexity translator is to convert your insights into a simplified but highly effective story to drive commitment and action. Communication is the ultimate test of complexity translating—your ability to bring all of your work together into a powerful narrative.

The narrative requires different versions, depending on the audience. For example, can you take a complex piece of research and insights (let's say a new business strategy for fixing a failing shoe company's entire brand line) and deliver versions for your CEO, for the board of direc-tors, for your direct reports, and for your peers? Tailoring what and how you communicate your story for each stakeholder group is paramount to being seen as a high potential.

Developing your storytelling skills. Synthesizing for storytelling is more than just having good speaking skills (writing skills are equally import-ant) and sharing a few examples. From extensive research on the topic, we know that the most effective narratives utilize a three-part structure

SKILLS THAT INCREASE YOUR VALUE AS AN INSIGHT INTEGRATOR

Data analysis skills. Learn as much as you can about statistics. Even if you don't consider yourself to be a math person, you need to have a working knowledge about the properties of different data characteristics.

Learn a computer language of some sort (it doesn't matter much which one, unless you want to program further). The discipline of learning Java, C++, Python, or SQL will help you align other types of data sources.

Practice your skills in asking questions and evaluating the various surveys and results of studies in the media. Questions such as "What was the margin of error on that study?" or "Were those results statistically significant and, if so, what was the strength of the relationship they found?" or even "What did they do to ensure this was a causal/predictive relationship and not simply a correctional/happenstance one?"

You don't have to be a statistics whiz, but you do need to understand enough to know when someone is using the wrong methods to draw conclusions. All these can help hone your skills, even if you will never be *the* data person.

Thematic skills. Creating theme or content summaries is a relatively simple skill to develop. Take a popular topic in the media and gather several different articles on the subject from distinctly different sources. While you are

---

highlighting a fundamental challenge or dilemma your organization is facing and how your initiative solves it.[1]

The following guidelines will help you build more compelling narratives to convey your translations of how to address these challenges and why your solution is the most attractive option:

1. Describe the problem or opportunity that your initiative addresses. Use what is called a "lede" in journalism. This attention-grabbing statement or two summarizes the challenge your audience is facing

reading them, keep a simple chart where you create lists of the five to seven themes you see, the questions columnists are asking, the philosophical issues raised, and legal implications. Then as you read (and reread as needed) each article, put a checkmark for each time the topic is mentioned. You will have a simple classification scheme as well as checkmark for how many times a particular theme was mentioned. Sum the numbers over the total (either total checks or total source materials, whichever will generate the most meaningful insights; these could be totally different numbers depending on the process), and you have a simple set of statistics.

Another method is to read texts, papers, and cases or view web clips of known points and counterpoints on key topics. Write a short summary while taking a position based on two or more sources. Share your framing with others and see what their reactions are and how they respond to the arguments, based on your summary. Have you captured the various sides or did you miss some key insights and themes? Is your summary compelling and comprehensive to others?

Financial skills. You need to develop moderate to strong financial skills, being able to read financial statements and understand how to break down a profit-and-loss statement, capitalization, Forex and Capex models, and so on. Either take a few online finance courses or find someone in your organization who can mentor you in finance.

and establishes clearly why your issue is also your audience's issue. Why should they personally be concerned or excited by the challenge? Define in simple but credible terms the key forces driving change that, in turn, lay the groundwork for why your initiative is needed. Illustrate these driving forces with concrete, relevant examples your audience is familiar with.

2. Explain the *dramatic conflict or fundamental challenge* your unit or organization will face if no action is taken. What will happen if your

initiative is not implemented? What opportunities will be forgone? Build your case with credible and vivid examples that your audience will understand and easily relate to.

3. Describe *how your solution or initiative resolves* the problem you captured in the opening of your narrative. Here you need to explain your solution in concrete terms and show how it successfully and elegantly addresses the problem or challenge. You can also offer an alternative solution that your audience might be aware of while explaining its shortcomings in contrast to yours. Summarize the *measurable outcomes* your solution will produce if implemented, along with a call to action in the form of initial steps and audience commitments.

Skills for adapting to your audience. Whether you are presenting one-on-one, addressing a large group of employees, or sharing an executive summary with senior leaders, you need to understand what will resonate with each group. Be prepared to adapt your content, speed of delivery, language, symbols, frameworks as well as the style you use to convey key messages. Promising managers often stumble because they are trapped in a prepared script, giving them no leeway to respond to curveball responses from their audiences.

Here are ways to get better at reading and adapting to your audience:

- When presenting in PowerPoint, hit the high notes and reinforce key points. Never read every bullet point or statement on the slide. Don't force your audience to read through each piece of information in sequence. Getting stuck in this point-by-point trap is a sure sign to others that you don't know your material well enough to have a real discussion. They'll actually interpret it as a sign that you're not ready to communicate with more senior audiences.

- Before every presentation, think carefully about how a specific audience typically looks at your issue. For example, does your boss think first and foremost about how your issue will affect costs or top-line growth or risk mitigation? Do your team members emphasize the impact on their own workload in relation to others, and who has accountability for results? Do certain peers look at the issue from an operational frame, worrying about how to most efficiently service customers? At the front end of each presentation to a specific audience, discuss the issue using its dominant frames, for example, the cost implications with the boss, the service implications for your team, and the efficiency issues with your peers.

- Open with a description of the *problem or opportunity* you're tackling rather than your solution, unless your boss asks otherwise. If you have done your homework before the presentation (and ideally had meetings in advance with key stakeholders), you will have learned there are shared perceptions about the problem. Starting with shared ground will get you initial buy-in to the thesis of your presentation. On the other hand, starting with your solution will often generate an opening debate about whether alternatives could work just as well.

- Hold one-on-one meetings with key decision makers ahead of the official decision meeting. We cannot stress this "pre-wiring" enough. Pre-wiring makes your stakeholders comfortable with how you will be framing the issue and helps you anticipate the tough questions they're likely to ask. Some stakeholders also need time to reflect. They don't appreciate being hit cold with new information in a decision-making meeting. One of us has two senior clients who react negatively to just about every idea on the first pass. They need the ideas in advance of every formal meeting to mull them over. Otherwise, they will derail any decision that favors the new idea.

- Ask colleagues who know a particular audience well what the likely reactions to your presentation's perspective and recommendations will be. What types of questions will they ask that could kill your recommendations? Once you have identified these killer questions, develop persuasive answers. One impressive high potential told us that he meets with the key audience members one-on-one before every important presentation. Using open-ended questions, he solicits their perspectives and solutions on his issue. He works to get agreement on what they see as the shared problem to solve and the most effective means of resolution. In his presentation, he then will voice the very opinions they shared, referencing their actual comments to him. In other words, he frames the issue in their voices and is transparent about including their input, making his position hard to contest. The recommendations are always a blend of his ideas and his stakeholders' suggestions. He is never surprised by a curveball question.

- When presenting, always observe your audience. Especially watch their body language: are they attentive, distracted, or scanning ahead through your handouts? Start each new slide by saying out loud, "I'm not going to hit all the points on this entire slide, but let me summarize the highlights." This can prompt you to focus more on your message and your audience's reaction to it and not on what's displayed on the screen or in a handout.

- Look for signals to speed up. See if people are flipping ahead in their handouts or looking at their watches or, worse, their phones. A technique that works with this type of audience is to know the five major points you wish to convey verbally for the meeting overall. If people are moving beyond where you are, jump to the next point ahead, if possible, or pull up the higher-level summary themes. Never read your slide deck or cover every point on that page or slide. Nothing is more painful than watching someone talk about points that have already been read and/or skipped over, while the senior executives are looking for the real meat of the discussion.

- Look for signals to slow down. Other audiences, in contrast, may need to linger on a single concept for a few minutes until they have assimilated your message. If you move too fast, you will be unable to build your case. They will think you are trying to cover up something you don't want to go into too deeply (not a good assumption for them to have) or are being disrespectful.

Focus on building flexibility into your own communications style and reading your audience well (somewhat similar to the concept of emotional intelligence but with an emphasis on communication).

Pitfalls. As with the other two steps in the process, storytelling has a few pitfalls:

- **Focusing only on the short or long term.** While the problem dictates the time span of your focus, one indicator of a high potential is whether you can step above the current level of content and see the longer and larger horizon. Similarly, if your story and recommended actions are too far into the future and not applicable today, you may be seen as too academic or disconnected from reality.

- **Delving into areas beyond the scope of the current problem.** Although demonstrating your breadth of knowledge and long-term strategic thinking is a must, if you include too many areas outside your scope, you will most likely signal a lack of focus or a failure to follow the parameters of the project. You might be seen as highly creative (organizational culture matters here), but usually you don't want to think too far afield.

- **Getting the data wrong or analyzing it incorrectly.** While this pitfall might seem better placed early on (and it certainly applies there as well), it's here for a reason: You need to know your domain first then obtain the right data. If your numbers or analysis approach have a major flaw, your entire proposal and story become suspect and probably will not progress further. If the decision meeting is with a senior executive, you may also damage your credibility permanently. This type of flaw in finance can cause a corporation to publicly restate its numbers. So you will be off the list for a promotion. Always be extra careful that what you collect, analyze, and share in your story is sound.

- **Making up a story with unsupported data.** If you want to skip the data and insights phases and go right to recommendations in your storytelling approach, you certainly can. However, if you get caught making it up, it's likely the end of the line for your potential.

- **Becoming more committed to the story than the data and insights.** If you collect the data, create an initial story, and then start to morph it over time into a highly exaggerated version with fantastic claims, you are setting yourself up for a credibility crash.

. . .

A complexity translator is a well-informed and compelling communicator, up, down, and sideways. Your ability to take in a wide range of data, discern critical insights, and then shape them into a narrative compels commitment and action. Be prepared to respond to disarming questions and be able to pivot your thinking in real time rather than simply defaulting to say, "Let me get back to you on that one."

Now we turn to the final X factor, the foundation for all the others. Catalytic learning enhances the other skills; the next chapter shows how.

Summary Lessons

- You have to become a master translator of the complex world around your organization for your stakeholders.

- By skillfully gleaning insights from information of all kinds, you must be able to cull and then call out the key ideas and priorities, and the best decision to make.

- To master complexity translating, you need to develop your skills in scanning for the right data, looking for patterns while integrating your insights into a coherent mental map, and then synthesizing the critical information into a powerful narrative.

- It is critical to read your audiences well, before you even enter the room where a decision is to be made. Understand their frames of reference, and the data and arguments that will resonate with them. Anticipate the questions that could "kill" your request.

- High potentials understand that even the narratives you construct must be adapted to the worldviews of the different constituents they are influencing.

6

Catalytic Learning

How to Turn Insights into Performance

Four of the five X factors—situation sensing, talent accelerating, career piloting, and complexity translating—differentiate high potentials from their peers and others. The fifth X factor that supports all the others is a mindset we call "catalytic learning."

Catalytic learning is learning with a purpose. It's what you do with what you're learning, how you take insights and lessons and convert them into performance. It's *catalytic* because this kind of learning transforms lessons into actions. High potentials learn quickly and understand how to apply that learning to benefit the organization.

In chapter 1, we mentioned that entrepreneur Elon Musk possesses one of the X factors in spades. It is catalytic learning. Musk has a bachelor's degree in physics and economics, but he was a long way from having the knowledge to build a spacecraft company when he started SpaceX. Musk literally taught himself rocket science by extensively reading applied textbooks and interviewing industry heavyweights. His passion for applied learning also paid off in another venture, Tesla. This same trait is found among world-class athletes whose quest to push their performance to new heights is fueled by their catalytic learning capacity.

The hallmark of the high potentials in our study is that they always find a way to get something out of every assignment. High-potential leaders see even the most daunting assignments as opportunities to push themselves and develop new knowledge and skills. They relish the idea of trying out different ideas, exploring functional areas where they might have no knowledge, testing and pushing the status quo, and taking on really tough challenges where they can grow as individuals and leaders. By being a catalytic learner, you send a message to your bosses, direct reports, and peers that you are willing, able, and excited to take on any new assignment. You can learn the most from each experience *and* deliver the results.

So, catalytic learning is all about what you do with each challenge. If you are a high potential, you are on an abiding quest to understand and proactively shape your environments. You have a desire to improve upon—or better yet, to transform—the status quo and yourself, even if the assignment or role is not quite what you had in mind.

Turning a Disappointing New Role into a Stepping-Stone for Promotion

After successfully delivering on his latest promotional campaign, Michael, a young marketing manager in the United States, was dubbed a high potential and identified for new stretch opportunities. Michael really wanted a promotion and felt he was ready. Because he had been with the company only two years, however, it was not willing to promote him to a director role so quickly, despite his success. Instead, his superiors wanted to see if he could deliver similar results with new clients and in a different cultural setting. So the company wanted to send him to Spain to try his hand there. He would still be in the marketing function, but the company told him he needed to move laterally to the business in Spain to build his international experience. The message to Michael was straightforward— do a good job, and we'll see about promoting you *after you deliver.*

Naturally, Michael was initially disappointed with this offer. He knew that the prior individual in the job had been a director, and yet the title he was being offered was at a lower level. Rather than react emotionally, turn it down, or even threaten to quit, Michael took a more measured and open-minded approach. He asked his colleagues and a mentor about the opportunity. Based on their feedback, he quickly concluded that, even if it didn't work out for him in the end, he'd learn some incredible new skills by spending a few years in Spain. In addition, he'd broaden his perspective through immersion in a wider geopolitical landscape and culture.

He decided to accept the position. He made his career interests known to his manager, of course, but he was careful not to overplay the importance of needing a promotion to director. Michael did not want to be seen as someone who was always "chasing the promotion" but instead focused on learning and growing his capabilities more broadly. As we discussed in chapter 2, he showed clever planning, leveraging his situation sensing skills.

Beyond just the politics of saying the right things to his supervisors, he had a great attitude, was excited about the new role, and showed it. When he arrived in Spain, Michael approached the position with an open mind and immediately dug into the nuances of the business. He made the right connections to the field organization early on. He quickly learned what would and would not translate from his work in the United States. He also demonstrated cultural savvy by observing others and modifying his more direct American style of communicating to fit into the accepted ways of working in Spain. He built relationships and focused on what was important to the people around him. He even became a *fútbol* fan and attended local matches with his colleagues. He focused on getting the work done, of course. In the end, Michael raised the bar on the marketing efforts in the local markets by applying his knowledge adapted from his time in North America. Nine months later, he was promoted to marketing director.

Michael demonstrated catalytic learning skills, showing his bosses that he could deliver in a totally new business environment, with different clients, and in a new cultural environment. He took the lateral position, converted all his new learning into performance, and ended up with a promotion. If he had walked away, he would have sent the wrong message about what was important to him. He might never have been given another chance for advancement.

Applying Learning to a Larger Role

Angelica was a superstar in the Latin American business of a shipping company. Like Michael, she needed some additional experience, but in this situation, the position was a lateral one at her organization's home operations in Texas. On the recommendation of her manager, she moved to a headquarters' role as a senior manager in operations. While she enjoyed setting policy and guidelines for safety and quality protocols and learning about the corporate culture, she struggled with the politics. She was less able to adapt her style to the home-office culture and within eighteen months was ready to return to Latin America. While her performance was solid, she did not exceed expectations. Her image was also somewhat tainted by her inability to really embrace the role. Many of her supporters had had high hopes for her as a future leader within operations.

After returning to the field organization, again in a lateral role, she began doing things differently. Her newfound understanding of how corporate worked helped her to better navigate and position the work she was doing locally. She had much greater knowledge of the quality agenda of the home-office operations function. She was able to connect the dots in ways that her colleagues could not and was instrumental in influencing the leaders in her region to collaborate with the enterprise-wide teams. She also now knew who to turn to at corporate for help. She had relationships with senior people who gave her their insights and provided air cover. The senior functional leaders recognized her impact almost immediately. In short, she applied her catalytic learning skills and upped her game when she returned to the field. Six months later, she was promoted into a larger regional role, and her high-potential status was reaffirmed. If you ask her today, she would tell you that while the home-office assignment was rocky and her success was limited, she learned much from the experience and it made her a much more influential leader.

Reflecting on the experiences of Angelica and Michael, what one piece of advice would we give you to become a high-potential leader? You have to find a way to learn from every experience and to keep learning throughout your career. Always assume with each assignment, whatever it may be, that you have something new to learn—a skill to master, new knowledge to gain, a lesson to learn or challenge to overcome, or a leadership capability to further refine and enhance. Deliberately practice the skills that you cannot do well and are demanded by each new situation and keep your core strengths always sharp and ready. Go out of your way to acquire today the knowledge for the future roles to which you aspire. As Debra Reed—CEO of Sempra Energy—notes, start early acquiring the knowledge essential to leading at the senior-most levels in your organization:

> I am an engineer by background, but at the start I knew it was important to understand how to make money in this industry. Earlier in my career, I was in HR and designed compensation plans that I had to present to our CEO. So I had to work closely with the controller and CFO. I really wanted to understand how the financial metrics were calculated. I invested a great deal of time with our controller learning our 10-K and 10-Q. Both are critical to get an understanding of what drives the financial outcomes of our business. I would sit down with the controller and raise lots of questions. I wanted to understand the key drivers, the risks. I invested hours and hours going on for years . . . I would go through the 10-Q every time it came out. I also went to outside courses. You can say that I am relentless in wanting to understand these things. I have always valued learning over knowing because learning gives you unlimited scope. Today I look for people who are putting forth this type of effort to improve themselves. I look for people who show the initiative before it is offered to them!

It All Starts with Learning Versatility

Catalytic learning is the kind of learning that can and should continue every day and in every experience you have throughout your personal and professional life. Book smarts are important, but so is the ability to see what is going on around you, acquire and synthesize new information (in a much broader way than we discussed in chapter 5), and adjust your behavior as a leader accordingly. Think of this in terms of *learning versatility*. The greater the versatility of your learning approach, the more successful you will be in your career and in life. If you are not open to learning and unable to apply your lessons, you will hit many stumbling blocks along the way. You might be able to overcome some, but others will stop you dead in your tracks.

Your Successes Can Impede Your Learning

In our work, we are repeatedly surprised to see individuals who actually don't learn or have stopped learning. The failure to stay a high potential over the long term is often the failure to learn new things that become imperatives. As you move up in your career, successes lead to promotion after promotion, and your track record encourages you to believe you've figured out the formula for success. This mindset leads you to underestimate the new demands you are facing or, worse, not even see them. As a result, you stop learning and eventually plateau or stumble.

In his book *High Flyers*, Morgan McCall Jr. points out: "Unfortunately, people often like the things that work against their growth. People like to use their strengths . . . to achieve quick, dramatic results, even if . . . they aren't developing the new skills they will need later on. People like to believe they are as good as everyone says . . . and not take their weaknesses as seriously as they might. People don't like to hear bad news or receive criticism . . . There is tremendous risk . . . in leaving what one does well to attempt to master something new."[1]

In researching executives who failed, Michael Lombardo and Robert Eichinger describe how the former strengths of these non-learners become serious liabilities: "Once [we] dug into this non-learning pattern, [the derailed executives'] strengths tipped over into overuses and weaknesses as they did more of what had previously been a good thing. The bright lorded it [their brightness] over others and missed getting new ideas, the organized became detail drones and missed the big picture, the creative had their fingers in too many pies and couldn't innovate, the aggressive over-managed and couldn't empower or build a team."[2]

One of our fast-track high-potential leaders stumbled precisely because his greatest strength became a liability as he progressed. Cole had built a reputation as a remarkable turnaround leader. By his mid-thirties, he could claim three highly successful turnarounds. Each one catapulted him higher on his company's high-potential list. He was on the verge of becoming the firm's youngest executive. Following his third turnaround, he stepped into his first major general manager's role. The style that he had honed for fast-paced firefighting, however, backfired completely in this role. Instead of delegating extensively and focusing on growth opportunities, Cole continued his habitual attention on short-term and seemingly urgent tactical problems, ones that he should have delegated. Unaccustomed to taking a long-term strategic perspective, he failed to invest in new products and instead worked on fine-tuning the mature ones. Within eight months on the job, his direct reports began grousing to Cole's superiors that he was micro-managing and lacked a true strategic perspective. At his year-end review, he learned that he had fallen off the high-potential list. The style and focus that had worked so well in his last three assignments had caused him to derail.

But Cole was also a catalytic learner. After this major setback, he rein-vented himself by focusing intensively on learning to delegate appropri-ately and to cultivate a strategic perspective. Two years later, he was back on the high-potential list headed toward the executive suite, but only after intense self-reflection, concerted long-term efforts at practice, and open-ness to personally challenging feedback.

When Lombardo and Eichinger looked at the other side of the coin—executives who sustained their high-potential status—they discovered that these executives had pronounced differences from their derailed peers. For example, those who were successful sought out *more feedback* on how they came across to others and what they needed to do to be better performers. They had approximately *twice the variety of leadership challenges* across their assignments (back to our herky-jerky career path) than their derailed peers. In essence, they had more learning experiences that gave

ARE YOU A CATALYTIC LEARNER?

As you read the following questions, ask yourself how many characterize the way in which you like to learn. The more that describe you, the more likely you are a true catalytic learner.

- What are your preferences for learning new things? Do you prefer formal methods (e.g., reading, classroom, online courses), informal methods (e.g., mentors, coaching, experiences), or both equally? Ideally, you'd enjoy both. Can you easily switch between different types of learning situations and environments?

- Do you conduct after-experience reviews to identify what you've learned from an assignment, project, or even a meeting and how you might link it to what you know and where it might apply in the future?

- Do you regularly seek feedback from others on what you are doing well and where you can improve? Do you truly listen to and absorb that feedback and do something concrete about it?

- Have you received feedback on your inherent strengths and blind spots and developed work-arounds to avoid getting derailed in the future? Do you know how and when to compensate for your shortcomings?

- Do you focus on both refining your strengths and developing your opportunity areas? Are you constantly experimenting in thoughtful ways with new approaches and behaviors? Do you set regular

---

them greater opportunities to build a broader repertoire of skills and perspectives. In response to these many unfamiliar situations, they *mastered new skills* and *expanded their ways of thinking*. As a result, they performed better than their peers because they consistently incorporated new capabilities into their leadership repertoires. The core differentiator was the high potential's *willingness* and *capacity to learn new competencies* in order to succeed in tough, first-time, and adverse circumstances.

learning goals for yourself—in terms of behavioral skills to master and new knowledge to acquire?

- Do you have a formal development plan that you update frequently as you successfully meet your goals?

- Do you approach new situations with a fresh pair of eyes every time or do you immediately jump to a solution and perspective that you've tried in the past? The former, of course, describes the catalytic learner.

- Do you consider the cultural context and the way people work and interact in each new role and adapt your style accordingly? Do you seek common ground to build relationships?

- Are you constantly scanning the business and social environment around you for cues as to what to learn and how to best adapt?

- Would others describe you as having low, medium, or high emotional intelligence? Do you enjoy figuring out other people in terms of what motivates them? Do you observe thoughtfully the nonverbal behavior of your colleagues and use your interpretations to improve your interactions?

- Can you identify the central players in each given situation? Do you look beyond job titles and expertise to observe who is talking to whom, who really seems to be in charge, and who has the greatest informal influence? Do you effectively build relationships with these individuals so you can learn the real dynamics of every situation?

Assessing Yourself

A good way to learn from every assignment (like Angelica and Michael) and avoid getting too stuck on your past successes (like Cole) is to ask yourself a few key questions as you move through each new assignment: Where and how do I need to adapt to this new situation? What underdeveloped skill must I cultivate? What new knowledge do I need to acquire? Who can help me understand what specifically I need to master and do differently from my prior assignment? How can I apply these learnings elsewhere in my organization? Once you start applying these learnings to new situations, you will be practicing catalytic learning.

Use the questions in the sidebar "Are You a Catalytic Learner?" as a starting point. The rest of this chapter focuses on specific advice for cultivating your catalytic learning skills.

How to Cultivate Your Catalytic Learning Skills

Catalytic learning is a quality you can cultivate with practice. It starts with your mindset. For example, most of the high potentials that we know deeply believe in the power of continuous improvement, whether in reinventing products or processes or themselves. As we noted, they appear to have a higher sensitivity to shortcomings in the status quo and to seeing opportunities emerging around them. For example, when we asked the partners in one professional services firm to identify their promising young high potentials, every individual they named was known for championing a unique initiative that significantly improved the organization. For those partners, potential was synonymous with thinking expansively about what is possible, not just what is doable.

What makes high potentials more sensitive to opportunities is curiosity, a desire to be innovative and a drive to be highly influential. It is not, however, the curiosity and drive of a deep specialist who wants to understand all the nuances of tax accounting or social media campaigns but rather of a generalist who wants to push the entire business agenda forward. High-potential leaders are broadly curious, which may explain why many move away from their original functional role over time. This breadth of curiosity serves them extremely well in the world of herky-jerky career paths (as discussed in chapter 4). As they literally leap from one functional area to another, they have to make a quick study of their new terrain. They have to demonstrate learning versatility to see the cues in the environment from all angles and rapidly apply that to how they are performing and working with others. Their preference for a breadth of learning also explains the capacity to excel in the X factor of complexity translating. Breadth of interests facilitates the capacity to more easily connect disparate data points.

But beyond curiosity and an essential discomfort with the status quo, you can and need to develop another dimension of catalytic learning. This is the type of mindset you bring to the table—a *fixed* or a *growth* mindset.

Practice a Growth Mindset

Carol Dweck, a psychology professor at Stanford University, was struggling to figure out why some students were caught up in proving their abilities to others, while other students simply learned and enjoyed themselves. From her observations, she discerned that people could be categorized by two different mindsets about their abilities. Which view you choose profoundly determines how you approach your goals and how you respond to risk and setbacks, both critical dimensions of career piloting skills.[3]

If you believe your personal qualities are more or less set in stone—the fixed mindset—you are more likely to be driven to prove yourself over and over: "Yes, I am smart enough to succeed at this." With a fixed mindset, however, you'll also fear serious challenges that could reveal what you perceive to be your inadequacies. In contrast, if you possess a growth mindset, you see big challenges as exciting opportunities to learn and grow. Your personal capabilities are not givens, but rather can be cultivated through your efforts. You believe you can do almost anything if you try deliberately and thoughtfully.

Dweck captured the real advantage of the growth over fixed mindset (italics ours): "It's not just that some people happen to recognize the value of challenging themselves and the importance of effort. Our research has shown that this comes directly from the growth mindset. When we teach people the growth mindset, with its focus on development, these ideas about *[the value of] challenge and effort follow* . . . When we put people in *a fixed mindset, with its focus on permanent traits,* they quickly fear challenge and devalue effort."[4]

The growth mindset of high potentials is not simply a focus on personal growth, but as we have noted, it is a desire to innovate and improve upon the status quo, along with a belief that any challenge or task can ultimately be accomplished. For example, in our interviews with high potentials, we frequently heard these types of comments: "I thrive on change," "I am always asking myself what needs improvement around here," "I look around and see so many opportunities to transform our work," "I love to get my team excited about doing things differently," "I love to create and build new things," "My favorite assignments involve leading innovation efforts."

When management thinker Jim Collins examined why certain companies thrived more than others in his book *Good to Great*, he observed that a distinguishing attribute was the type of leader who, in every case, led his or her company to be exceptional over time.[5] They were self-effacing individuals with strong growth mindsets. From our standpoint, what makes these growth-mindset leaders so effective is the impact they have on their teams and organizations. Research has shown that members of growth-mindset groups are much more likely to share their candid opinions and constructively disagree with one another. The advantage, of course, is that they explore problems in greater depth and breadth. They learn from mistakes and setbacks and alter their tactics and strategies adroitly. They maintain a healthy level of confidence and end up more productive than those with a fixed mindset. In fixed-mindset groups, productive and open discussions are rarer because they are perceived to have the potential to reveal an individual's shortcomings.

In one study, business school students working in fixed- and growth-mindset groups on a complex organization simulation demonstrated these extreme differences in outcomes.[6] Each group was purposely given very high production standards to meet, so high that both groups consistently fell short in their early attempts. Those with the growth-mindset orientation, however, kept learning. They assessed their setbacks, listened to feedback, and then altered their strategies. Despite a grueling simulation, they maintained a healthy sense of optimism and confidence. They finished up being far more productive than the fixed-mindset teams. The latter found it hard to learn critical lessons from their setbacks and, in turn, persevere.

Some researchers have argued that Dweck's approach to a growth versus fixed mindset applies to those early in their careers, but that it falls short of reality for midcareer or senior leaders. Thanks to experience, the latter have a firm and often well-grounded understanding of their strengths and opportunity areas. It's also hard to argue that your mindset and level of effort matter more than your actual tangible results. Trying really hard with more innovative ideas to drive sales in a difficult region filled with competitors is admirable. But if you don't deliver on your plan, you will still get dinged on your performance review (which is, by definition, a fixed-mindset approach). That's the reality of the workplace where effort only counts if you end up with achievements. So the simpler notions of a growth mindset—keep trying harder and be innovative—have limits as you climb. That said, if you don't approach your work with a positive, open-minded, and feedback-receptive attitude, you are unlikely to deliver your best results or ever get any better at anything. Clearly, having a growth mindset is reflected both in where you are coming from (your personality and inherent skills) and in how you choose to engage going forward.

A growth mindset as it relates to catalytic learning is about having an expansive perspective—an openness to thinking broadly about business and people. It's about being a versatile learner and taking advantage of all opportunities to learn and grow. It's about using newly acquired knowledge and skills to drive improvements in the business where others might not or have not. Cultivating a growth mindset is a critical component of catalytic learning.

Approach Setbacks with Optimism

Related to Dweck's growth mindset is the idea that optimism leads to learning. Remember the case of Michael; his positive attitude helped him be successful in the new role in Spain and that in turn (along with other X factors) resulted in his promotion. Optimism leads to many positive outcomes, which include an appetite for learning. If your worldview is one of possibilities, you are more likely to visualize your success and therefore obtain it. If you take a negative perspective, everything just seems to go wrong for you. It's easy to get depressed and frustrated, and lose your motivation to achieve, let alone deliver the basics.

In our discussions with senior leaders, they always talked about the positive energy coming from the high potentials they remembered most. High potentials possess a baseline disposition that is essentially optimistic. This disposition gives the high potential several critical advantages. Their optimism blunts or dampens the fear of failure, encourages perseverance and experimentation, and also prevents anxiety and rumination. For example, when faced with choices about where to invest in new products or services, do you find this challenging decision engaging and then look forward to its outcome? Or do you obsess first about making the right decision and then worry afterward whether you made the right one?

In contrast, those who are not high potentials may more often focus on downside risks, especially those that could translate into setbacks to their careers. They are more prone to finding reasons why *not* to challenge the status quo. Or why a problem is intractable and then what (or whom) to blame for why they could not take action. They may end up more pessimistic in tough situations, or at the least too painfully realistic. So their personal mission is to simply get through a tough assignment, wait for the next opportunity, or blame others or external events for their inability to get traction.

Martin Seligman, psychology professor at the University of Pennsylvania, discovered that pessimism leads people to give up too quickly.[7] Pessimists rarely persist in the face of tough challenges and therefore fail more frequently, even when success is attainable. In contrast, optimism breeds perseverance and experimentation. While Seligman studied the power of optimism across a wide variety of contexts, his research in one particularly challenging profession—life insurance sales—has parallels to our work with high-potential leaders. Selling insurance is one of the toughest jobs around. You spend most of your day cold-calling people who consistently reject you. The job is so demoralizing that more than 50 percent of new agents quit by the end of their first year. Seligman was curious to see what role optimism played in explaining an agent's success over time. Could optimism determine the performance potential of a sales agent?

In one research project, he measured the optimism levels of two hundred experienced insurance agents. He chose half because they were very productive agents and half who were not nearly as productive. He discovered that the most optimistic agents sold 37 percent more insurance, on average, in their first two years than those who scored as more pessimistic. Even more remarkably, agents who scored in the top 10 percent of optimism sold 88 percent more than their counterparts in the most pessimistic tenth. Optimism proved a critical contributor to performance over time.

The more surprising finding came in Seligman's special force study at Metropolitan Life. Here he selected a group of over hundred agents who had failed—note the word *failed*—the industry's standard test but had scored in the top half of his assessment for optimism. No one else would hire these agents; they couldn't pass the baseline exam. The agents were not aware, however, that they had been identified as highly optimistic individuals or that they were in a special study. So how did these "losers" perform? In their first year, they outsold their more pessimistic colleagues in the regular sales force by 21 percent and by 57 percent in the second year. They also outsold the average agent in the regular sales force by 27 percent by their second year. They even sold as much as the optimists in the regular force. From these results, Seligman concluded that optimism matters. While talent and motivation should be at least as important as persistence, it turns out that, over time, the rejections pile up, and the persistence a person's optimism generates becomes decisive. Imagine yourself as a high-potential leader driving change in a large, complex organization. How many setbacks are you likely to face? Optimism becomes your best defense to learn and persist.

But optimism has a second advantage. It promotes a positive and empowering energy that is contagious with your team. The high potential's organization is energized to tackle very challenging situations with greater conviction and confidence. A series of studies have shown that your disposition is contagious particularly if you have a formal leadership role. If you bring an optimistic attitude into your team meetings, the positive energy will affect the mood of the participants. They will be more open to experimenting, learning, implementing, and innovating in the face of setbacks. Similarly, if you have a pessimistic mood, the team dynamic will turn into a sense of defeat, playing it safe, or worse, cynicism.[8]

High-potential leaders are not, however, dreamers. Their optimism is tempered by a pragmatic mindset. As individuals, they have cultivated a strong tactical side, thinking carefully about short- and long-term practical steps as well as contingencies. When we observe them leading difficult change efforts, they always realistically describe how challenging the path to success will be for their teams. At the same time, they express their optimism and confidence in the rewards of the destination goals and in their team's capabilities to achieve them.

Raise Your Level of Self-Awareness and Reflection

One very important tactic for building your skills in this X factor of catalytic learning is to enhance your overall self-awareness by reflecting on the situation around you and what you have just learned. Too many people rarely step back and consider what has just happened. Whether after a short meeting with your boss's boss or a customer, a six-month-long project, or a two-year assignment in Shanghai, you need to build your skill at reflection. Ask yourself, "What did I see happen in that meeting and why—what made it productive, what made it less productive, what would I do differently in hindsight?" "What did I learn from that project and what could I have done better or worse?" "What are the strengths and weaknesses that I keep seeing myself exhibit over and over again, and which areas do I seem to be getting better at?" "What was I trying to get out the assignment and did I achieve that outcome?" "Why am I acting this way today and how is it affecting the quality and productivity of my work and relationship outcomes?"

These questions will help you build your own self-awareness and hone your skills in learning from your experiences. If you are going to be a catalytic learner and a high potential, you must be able to reflect on everything quickly and crystallize that information for yourself. Some people use a journal—the tech-savvy ones use an electronic tablet—to capture their observations and reflections (almost like a diary), while others keep it all in their head. Others find reflection partners for specific tasks or skills. Those who are the most effective at reflection have built it into their calendars. One of our high-potential exemplars, Jim, explains how he uses his three protected windows of daily reflection time:

> I block out on my calendar three hours every day when there can be no meetings and minimal interruptions—9–10 a.m., 12–1 p.m., and 4–5 p.m. My assistant and staff know that no one can book time with me during these hours. The only exception would be my superiors. I use the 9 a.m. window to do work that requires a great deal of concentration and reflection. I also use it to do forward thinking about what I need to accomplish. I keep a simple journal of my daily, quarterly, and annual to-dos that I review to be certain that all my actions are aligned. I use the 12–1 p.m. hour to build relationships. I have a list of relationships that I need to cultivate. So I do four networking lunches a week. My last protected hour is to reflect backwards—what did I intend to accomplish, what actually happened. Every other week, I take some of this protected time to review my team, their performance, and their deliverables. I ask myself what I wish they were doing better, what would help them perform better, and how is my relationship with each of them. The latter has proven to be very important. By making my relationships better, their performance has visibly improved. They are also more open to my feedback. It's been a virtuous cycle.

The process of reflecting and codifying what you are learning is what will help you the most. It will also help you to develop those who work for you. If you can easily articulate the important outcomes of your various activities and experiences, you will certainly be able to explain why different roles are important for your team members. This is a vital role that leaders play for their organization.

Build a Strategic Network

You can become a stronger catalytic learner by cultivating a strategic network of others around you. Professor Rob Cross and Accenture's Robert Thomas were curious whether high-potential leaders networked differently in comparison to their peers.[9] Perhaps they had larger networks? Or perhaps they concentrated all of their efforts on building deep relationships with more powerful people? It turned out that neither was the real differentiator.

They learned that large networks can cause you to stumble. You can spend too much of your time with your colleagues and external networks rather than getting your work done. If you concentrate too much on powerful people, you end up with far fewer sources for critical information from the bottom of the organization. When implementing initiatives, you don't have enough relationships on the ground to help you out. Furthermore, your peers don't trust you after watching how much time and energy you spend managing impressions and sucking up to bosses (remember our cautionary statements in chapter 2 regarding situation sensing).

Instead, Cross and Thomas discovered that the high potentials had diverse yet selective networks. Beyond helping them to be more influential, they relied on these networks to broaden their expertise, learn new skills, and find meaning and purpose in their work. For example, they had strong ties to individuals who offered them new information or expertise. As a result, they gained more insights into markets, the issues of other functions and divisions, and politics. So they became better at complexity translating and career piloting. They also did a far better job of sharing best practices and contacts from other industries that, in turn, inspired them to undertake innovations in their organizations. They did, however, cultivate links to powerful people who provided mentoring, political support, and resources; helped with coordinating projects and garnering support from the rank and file; and made sense of events within and outside the organization. But they never did so to the exclusion of building relationships with their peers or those more junior. As a result, they didn't lose credibility with colleagues, in contrast to managers who spent most of their time networking with superiors. Equally important, the high performers had individuals who gave them developmental feedback—pushing them to be better and challenging their perspectives and decisions. In other words, their networks served as sources of catalytic learning. That is exactly what your networks should be doing for you. Maritta, a seasoned high potential participant in our research, captured the importance of this network or what she calls her "development board":

> Every place I've worked, I always had two types of relationships . . . people who are giving me day to day mentoring and sponsorship and more senior people to whom I can turn for bigger picture advice. In my current role, I have five individuals from whom I seek developmental advice. For example, Ru really knows how to think through people problem issues. So when someone on my team is underperforming, I reach out to Ru for brainstorming about whether to coach and what's the best approach. Joyce, on the other hand, completes a lot of my blind spots around communications. For example, our CEO asked me to do a "lessons learned" on a major project. Joyce was my sounding board as I prepared. She is also politically savvy helping me navigate certain minefields that could have come up in the presentation. In return, Joyce and Ru come to me for coaching in areas where I am strong or where they just need a confidential sounding board.

Find Your Energizers and Truth Tellers

One somewhat surprising conclusion from Cross and Thomas's research was the importance of having energizing people in your network. These individuals always see opportunities, even in challenging situations—back to our discussion of optimism. They help you realize your aspirations. Years ago, one of us interviewed the founder of Priceline, Jay Walker. He attributed a portion of his success to finding the right brainstorming partners. He would take his wild ideas to the individuals who would help him build and refine his ideas into viable businesses. They would safeguard his enthusiasm for an idea while simultaneously helping him find ways to tactically implement a more realistic version of his wild idea. He explained that such partners were hard to find. The average individual will tell you all the ways your idea will not work.

You also need truth tellers in your network. Greg Veith, a high-potential director at Microsoft, ensures that he has "Greg whisperers" to help him reflect on his insights and leadership style by providing candid feedback. They balance his natural inclination to be very enthusiastic about what is possible in the big picture. They help him test out his initiatives before they actually get implemented and gauge engagement at all levels of his organization. Veith explains:

> I like to chase big opportunities. So I need whisperers to help me see what an opportunity will look like from a pragmatic perspective. I am always soliciting feedback from my team members: "What am I missing, what are my blind spots?" "What outcomes are at risk if we do this and not that?" "Can we absorb the cost of new work with the existing people?" One of my direct reports sets a high bar on execution. They help me see the resourcing and implementation trade-offs, any roadblocks, pushes our standards, and keeps me on top of critical details. I have a whisperer who is my rhythm of the business and process person. They help me answer the questions: "What's our six-month road map?" "Are we on budget?" "How are our finances overall?" "Is our head count too high or low?" A couple others on my team help me understand the feedback "on the street." For example, I learned that I needed to spend more time just meeting with our individual contributors. So now I schedule once-a-week lunches with about six people on the team and just shoot the breeze, get to know them personally, and answer questions they have. I rely on one of my whisperers who is very observant about people's body language. They help me read-the-room, and identify who to follow up with after a meeting.

In contrast to these whisperers and energizers are the de-energizers or "Debbie Downers," as popularized by *Saturday Night Live*. These folks are quick to point out the obstacles you'll face with any initiative and find all the reasons why your ideas won't work. They also like to critique people and sometimes lack real concern for others. Cross and Thomas suggest that you reshape your role to avoid these people, work to change their behavior, or simply desensitize your reactions to them so you don't dwell on their impact.

Practice Deliberately

Research in the field of expertise reveals that you have to continually extend the reach and range of your skills.[10] Experts who attain high levels of performance instead often fall into the trap of responding automatically to situations. After all, they are the experts and so come to rely on and believe in their intuition based on past experiences. But trusting your gut when encountering an *unfamiliar* situation is unlikely to work to your advantage. Rather, you need to practice gaining new perspectives, skills, and knowledge; reflect on your experiences; seek feedback; and analyze your outcomes. Here is where deliberate practice comes in.

Deliberate practice requires that you identify an underdeveloped skill that will be in high demand in your new role or important transition. Then practice that skill—*deliberately.* As K. Anders Ericsson and his colleagues point out, a wide variety of experts dedicate several hours daily to deliberate practice.[11] World-class violinist Jascha Heifetz said, "The discipline of practice every day is essential. When I skip a day, I notice a difference in my playing, after two days, the critics notice, and after three days, so does the audience."[12] We mentioned in our introductory chapter a senior manager who was on everyone's succession list to become the firm's CEO. Beyond his outstanding performance, deliberate practice was his differentiating activity.

Yet, the vast majority of managers and executives expend hardly any time on skill development, given the meetings and day-to-day tactical demands that consume their days. Because of these very demands, you should focus on developing only one or two skills at a time. When you achieve a degree of mastery, then you can begin to work on the next. You need also to carve out specific days, times, and locations for your practice, otherwise meetings, emails, and day-to-day demands will waylay your efforts. Determine precisely what underdeveloped but needed skill demands your attention now. Reach out and confirm your choice with colleagues who are keenly aware of the dynamics of your new assignment and your skill sets and gaps.

The story of Juan Ramón Alaix, CEO of the pharmaceutical firm Zoetis, illustrates the lengths to which a high-potential leader will go to become outstanding.[13] As he was preparing to assume the CEO job, he knew that he lacked the sophisticated communications skills that the role would demand. To prepare, he undertook a demanding eighteen-month training program. He began with a series of assessments to determine skill gaps that would be most relevant to his upcoming CEO role. He then found an experienced CEO who mentored him on specific aspects of the job where he lacked experience. Together, on a two-day retreat, they explored how the CEO role differed from his past general management positions. They talked about the specific stakeholders who would influence Zoetis's future success and how best to communicate with each. They continued these conversations once a month. Reflecting on these meetings, Alaix commented:

> Between running the business and planning for the IPO [of Zoetis from Pfizer], I could easily have avoided the work of preparing for the CEO job on the grounds that I was too busy. Having regular appointments with my mentor prevented that. It was also valuable to have an outsider listen to my concerns and challenge me to think differently. When you're a business leader, your time is often spent mostly with colleagues and subordinates, and you miss the challenge of an independent opinion. My mentor raised issues I hadn't considered. He would ask questions and challenge me to examine my choices. These structured conversations forced me to do a disciplined analysis to answer his questions.[14]

But Alaix did not stop there. He hired a communications expert from whom he learned the different formats in which a CEO needs to communicate. He learned how to do television and print interviews, deliver a keynote address, present to small groups, hold one-on-one conversations with a key investor, and handle the scripted and Q&A parts of an earnings call. He would later hire a second trainer who joined his team to observe him in meetings, town halls, and investor forums, and provided ongoing feedback.

While the investment was high and intensive, Alaix saw its critical role in his later success as a CEO. In reflecting on his investment in training, he observed:

> A lot of people, when they reach a certain age, are reluctant to accept training. That's not true for me—I'm very open to it. I'd had communication training over my career, but the preparation for our IPO was much more intensive. Before I did my first TV interview, for instance, I probably spent more than eight hours doing mock interviews. I believe that the key to success in communication is preparation. By the time I gave the first road-show pitch to investors, I'd rehearsed it at least 40 times . . . Every leader has a recipe for success. For me, preparation is most important. I believe in over-preparing, even though it's time consuming. Part of preparation is being humble enough to accept feedback. The time I spend getting ready for a challenge and the openness I have to coaching are investments that always pay me back.[15]

. . .

We've now examined all five of the X factors that differentiate high potentials: situation sensing, talent accelerating, career piloting, complexity translating, and catalytic learning. All five skills are central to being recognized as a high potential in your organization. However, they aren't enough.

Every organization has particular processes it uses to determine who is, and who isn't, a high potential. But, as we explained in chapter 1, these organizational processes are often shrouded in mystery, if not deliberate secrecy. We now turn to the topic of what exactly goes on in that black box. In the next three chapters, we will show you how to make sense of and navigate your organization's high-potential processes. We begin with a deep dive into how your organization assesses whether or not you are high-potential talent.

Summary Lessons

- The greater the learning versatility you can demonstrate in adjusting behavior and mindsets to new situations, the more successful you will be in your career and in life. High potentials learn from many different kinds of events or experiences and apply those insights to future situations. They have the ability to quickly synthesize and use information and insights in new ways and to shift their behaviors to the right approach demanded by each circumstance.

- Practice enhancing your overall self-awareness by reflecting on the situation around you and what you have just learned. Find colleagues who can be your reflection partners.

- Build networks of relationships to broaden your expertise, learn new skills, and find purpose in your work. Share best practices and contacts from other industries. Cultivate links to senior leaders who can provide mentoring, political support, resources, and help coordinate projects.

- Given the work demands on your time, focus on only one or, at most, two skills to develop at a time. When you achieve a degree of mastery, begin to work on the next.

- Build in dedicated time on specific days, times, and locations for your deliberate practice. Otherwise, meetings, emails, and day-to-day demands will waylay your efforts.

- Solicit guidance from colleagues who have a keen sense of the assignment dynamics you face ahead. Ask them to recommend where you should make development investments and to provide you with ongoing feedback.

PART TWO

How to Navigate Your Organization's High-Potential Processes

7

Assessment

How Your Organization Sizes You Up

We turn now to one of those organizational black boxes that few employees understand—the formal assessment process. Every organization uses some kind of structured assessment process to identify its high potentials and choose among them for filling the top jobs. We will look at how this mysterious process actually works and how you can influence it. We turn our attention to the advantages of the different assessment tools, how each are deployed to assess you, and how you can influence their outcomes.

Why Organizations Use Data-Based Assessments

Many firms turn to industrial-organizational psychologists and consultants to help them make informed decisions and to augment their internal talent processes. They collect data through formal tools, assessments, simulations, structured interviews, and psychological tests to influence decisions about who are the true high potentials in their organization. While they also use many of these tools for individual development purposes (and Allan Church and Christopher Rotolo's benchmark research indicates that this is the most common use by far), organizations also deploy them for talent reviews, raising the stakes higher.[1] The assessment tools level the playing field for everyone being measured, assuming they are valid and implemented correctly.

For example, even if you tend to be less extraverted than others and have to work harder at the X factor of situation sensing with your boss, assessment feedback can reveal how effective you really are at building relationships with your direct reports and peers. An assessment tool might indicate that you have tremendous potential to lead at more strategic levels, even if the senior leaders haven't seen you yet demonstrate this capacity. It may provide just the right piece of data they need to put you into that bigger role. But there are more advantages to these tools.

Correcting Outdated or Negative Impressions of You

Assessments help correct negative perceptions by showing either that you actually don't have a perceived shortcoming or that you have significantly improved a weakness. So the data can help reverse (or offset) these negative perceptions and reinforce positive ones. Assessments, in other words, can give you a new start.

Lacey was a high-potential and super-smart young manager in sales. She had been a star as an individual salesperson, but her ambition blinded her to the necessity of developing relationship skills in a management role. Her peers saw her as overly aggressive and not collaborative, and she couldn't stop herself from competing with everyone that she came into contact with. Lacey positioned herself to take credit for every positive sales outcome, as if each success was all her own work.

After peers assessed her via a 360-degree survey and gave her negative feedback as hypercompetitive, she decided it was important to change her behavior. She knew she needed to get better if she wanted to remain a high potential. In essence, she taught herself to stop reacting to everything with a knee-jerk need-to-win mentality. She focused on seeing the bigger picture and understanding the need to bring her peers along. When the team achieved a sales target, she ensured that she shared recognition with them.

After about six months of learning to behave more cooperatively, she found herself in much better working relationships with her peers and direct reports (as they had experienced the negative downstream implications of her competitive actions with others as well). Despite this improvement, the word on the street was that she was still not a team player. Many of her former colleagues had moved on to new roles and had not directly experienced her improved working style.

Perhaps, over time, these perceptions of her would change for the better, but in the short term, they would have continued to be an issue in talent review discussions if she had not participated in a follow-up 360-degree assessment. This second survey was conducted specifically for her upcoming talent review meeting (and to determine her place on the slate for a new role). The results highlighted her significant improvement in demonstrating collaborative behaviors. This documented change enabled her to get promoted much more quickly than she would have if her company's leaders had relied solely on existing impressions.

Identifying Leading Indicators of Your Future Potential

Companies can also use assessment tools to identify leading indicators of future potential. For example, through applied research methods, organizations can determine a core capabilities profile to predict the future potential of more junior talent. PepsiCo has such a program in place as part of its broader Leadership Assessment and Development or LeAD suite of programs. The early-career version, called the Potential Leader Development Center (or PLDC) consists of standard and customized tools, including cognitive, personality, situational judgment, and biographical data questions that statistically predict potential success.[2] PepsiCo offers the program to thousands of employees each year early in their career. In the spirit of transparency, it shares the results regarding how far they can go in their careers to the participants, their managers, and HR. The feedback is presented in the form of two leadership strengths and two leadership opportunities, and an indicator of future potential called a LIFT score (based on four levels of scoring). The term LIFT was chosen over the word "potential" to communicate to employees that everyone can develop greater leadership capability. Only about 17 percent of employees during each cycle (somewhere between two thousand and three thousand employees a year) achieve "Very Great LIFT," which indicates they have the highest potential to succeed in more senior roles. Others have "Great," "Moderate," or "Some" LIFT based on their results.

While this data is very useful to PepsiCo, what is perhaps most surprising and encouraging is that over 70 percent of employees who participated in the PLDC are satisfied with the feedback program overall. Their level of satisfaction did not vary significantly by how well they performed. In other words, employees (at least those early in their career) want to know where they stand and how far they can go in the company based on an objective assessment of important capabilities. If your company had such a program, would you opt out of the process or would you want to know your own level of potential for success? If you did less well than others (e.g., in a low or moderate group), what would you do about it?

At PepsiCo, even some percentage of those employees with the lowest categories of LIFT are promoted each year. But those with the highest levels based on the assessment are promoted at more than twice the average rate.[3] So, the high potentials see direct benefits from participating.

In sum, organizations can use assessment data in many ways and at different levels in your career. In the early stages, the data can serve as a leading indicator of your potential and help you focus on areas for development. At more senior levels, the data can inform decisions, provide missing information, assess for changes or improvements in development needs, or simply help compare candidates on some key skills or capabilities. Regardless, these types of data, whether in the form of a survey, test, online simulation, live interview, group exercise, or an all-day assessment center, can make or break your high-potential status.

Can I Influence the Outcomes of Assessments?

Overall, there are many different types of tools and processes, and each is best suited to measure different types of traits, skills, and characteristics. We know from the benchmark research that Church and Rotolo conducted with over eighty marquee companies known for their strong talent management practices that 360-degree feedback, personality assessments, and interviews are by far the most commonly used tools.[4] But other tools such as cognitive abilities tests, situational judgement, and simulations are also used as part of a broader battery of measures to assess for high potential in many organizations. In fact simulations, particularly those done online, are steadily rising in popularity—in part because of their ability to be customized to reflect unique business challenges. We'll take a look at why more companies are now using simulations to assess people's skills and then turn to the other commonly used tools. We'll examine what each tool measures and the ways in which you can (or cannot readily) influence the data obtained.

Simulations

If your organization is considering you for high-potential status, it will likely ask you to participate in a simulation. A simulation can be a simple online application, almost like a game, where you assume the persona of someone who has a major role (for example, a business leader in the field, a new CEO, a newly elected government official, the new senior vice president of marketing) and who faces some challenging situations. Or a simulation can be an all-day affair in which you role-play either one-on-one with a trained facilitator (this can be done in person or using technology) or in larger groups and are observed to see how you behave in different situations. Some newer simulations are games in disguise, but they test your leadership skills and capabilities. For example, a deep-space exploration game in which you determine outposts to colonize, build up resources, and launch different types of science missions might test your strategic thinking and operations skills. Or, a war-game simulation in which you choose players to ally with and engage in combat might be evaluating communications between you and your peers to determine how you approach teamwork and collaboration. Or, a football game where you participate in scouting, drafting players, and assigning starters might measure your talent management skills.

Whatever the approach, the basic premise is the same—novel situations (presented the same way to each participant who goes through the process) with specific types of outcomes that can be evaluated. Because simulations assess your ability to address challenges that you have not seen before, the assessors can consider your ability to think and process information. The results theoretically can help answer the question of whether you can engage in certain types of behaviors or how you think when responding or engaging with others.

How to ace a simulation test. If you've never had the opportunity to showcase your excellent skills at career piloting, a simulation could be a perfect chance for you to shine. Given that simulations are often conducted in real time (even if completed remotely on a computer or tablet), it is difficult to influence the outcome directly, other than by simply doing well in general. Unless you cheat somehow and find out in advance what the simulation is testing for (not recommended for ethical reasons), how else can you ensure you have the best chance of doing well?

First, devote the appropriate amount of energy and focus. Whether it is an online simulation you do on your own or a full-day assessment, put aside all other distractions. The more distracted and disrupted you are, the less focus you will have, which, in turn, can undermine your performance.

Revisit the X factors and the leadership and/or functional competencies your organization values. These can sometimes be embedded in the simulation. In addition, learn beforehand what your executive team sees as the key business drivers for your firm. These are typically pressing challenges that organizational leaders have to address to ensure the successful execution of strategic and cultural priorities. For example, they could be expanding the strategic focus towards greater organic growth or instilling a stronger culture of attracting and retaining talent. As we discussed in chapter 2 on situation sensing, the more you know about what is important to your organization and its cultural imperatives (chapter 9), the better off you'll be in the simulation. If you happen to know that a certain baseline level of financial acumen is important for more senior levels, regardless of the function you are in, it would be wise to read *Finance for Dummies* in advance and brush up on how to read a P&L statement and your organization's Form 10-K. The extent to which you can demonstrate knowledge of finance in real time (or in the simulation), the more likely you will be seen as a high potential. If the simulation involves other people (as in a group session), be on your best behavior, even when stressed. Stress may be exactly what the assessors are testing you on. After making decisions and preparing to present them, how do you behave when the entire situation changes on a dime? Do you get flustered, anxious, mad, inarticulate, unable to readjust course in real time? These are the types of behaviors and skills the simulation measures.

While organizations use simulations to gain insight into how you'll act in novel situations, they also want more information on how you typically act in daily situations and how others in the organization perceive those actions. This is where the 360-degree assessments come in.

360-Degree Feedback Surveys

The ever-popular 360-degree feedback surveys provide data on how others see you in the workplace. They measure perceptions of your current behavior and are less about your potential per se. Usually, the assessment questions are based on a leadership competency model, a set of organizational values, and/or dimensions considered important to effective leadership (similar to what we will cover in chapter 9, corporate culture). Because these surveys are so prevalent, the data is used to round out the information from talent reviews of influencing skills, relational leadership capabilities, competence at setting a mission, vision, strategy, ability to motivate and engage subordinates, collaboration skills, and so on.

Once ratings from your colleagues are collected, you receive the feedback in terms of how others see you in the aggregate on a specific dimension or competency. These are broken down by the behaviors associated with that particular competency across each group of raters. The raters typically include your manager, along with your peers, subordinates, and sometimes other groups such as customers. Given their significance to your career, your boss's ratings are often not anonymous, whereas the others' confidentiality is protected. This affords bosses the opportunity to be honest if they choose. Thus, if you behave differently with your boss, subordinates, and peers, your 360-degree survey will likely reveal these differences.

There are also self-ratings in which you rate your own behavior as you perceive it on a day-to-day basis. The degree of congruence or similarity between your own ratings and your colleagues' ratings is called "managerial self-awareness."[5] *In the field of psychology, research indicates that highly self-aware leaders deliver better performance and possess greater future potential.* So, ideally, your scores would be closely matched to those of your raters across the many dimensions being assessed (both on the strengths and opportunity areas). The more out of alignment your scores are with your raters' perceptions, the less self-aware and ultimately less effective you are as a leader.

How to select your raters. Because others are rating you, influencing the tool directly to improve your scores is difficult. While some people try to select only their friends and allies as raters, hoping for more favorable scores, this strategy can backfire quite easily. Many 360-degree survey processes include your bosses' review (or even require an approval) of your choice of raters, so you can easily get caught trying to cheat. And you may think your friends will rate you well, but they may not. Sometimes they feel they need to give you honest feedback because they are trying to help you become a better leader. The best advice for getting accurate and useful 360-degree data is to ensure you have selected a good range of individuals who work closely with you on a regular basis and who represent a breadth of perspective.

A standard part of the process in some 360-degree systems is to discuss your rater selection with your boss. If you don't align with your boss on the chosen raters, she and others in the talent review meeting may dismiss your results because they perceive bias on your part. They will see the difference between asking only your friends and those who will be tough but fair in their feedback as a difference in your courage, character, and leadership. In contrast, individuals who shy away from developmental feedback are rarely seen as high potentials.

By being proactive and thoughtful about your raters, you will demonstrate your openness to feedback and willingness to learn from the process. These signs of being a high-potential leader will be noticed. High potentials are supposed to seek feedback and learn from the results, not hide from it.

How companies use 360-degree results. Roger, Joy, and Victoria are three candidates who are being considered for a new role in the Asia Pacific region. The job requires setting the strategy and driving a growth agenda in a new business venture with a different culture and employee base from their parent company. All three candidates recently completed a 360-degree feedback assessment. A summary of their results by each of their organization's eight key leadership competencies is presented in table 7-1. The results represent the average ratings they received from their direct reports and peers combined. Normally, these would be separated, but for ease of interpretation we have combined them and used shading to illustrate their ranking. Dark shading is a clear strength (i.e., where they scored above the norm). No shading is a clear opportunity for their development (i.e., where they scored below the norm), and medium shading is about average.

When you look at the data in absence of anything else, you might rank-order the candidates by strengths and, therefore, place Victoria (with five strengths) first, followed by Roger (with four), and then Joy (with only two) last. In thinking through the requirements of the role, however, the decision requires more thought. The ideal high-potential candidate for the Asia Pacific role requires a blend of strategic and execution capability.

TABLE 7–1

360-degree results for three leadership candidates

Leadership dimension	Roger	Joy	Victoria
Strategic thinking	Weakness	Average	Strength
Setting direction	Strength	Average	Weakness
Operational savvy	Strength	Average	Weakness
Inspiring others	Strength	Weakness	Strength
Global mindset	Weakness	Average	Strength
Collaborating in a matrix	Strength	Average	Strength
Acting with integrity	Average	Average	Strength
Learning orientation	Weakness	Strength	Average

☐ Weakness   ▦ Average   ■ Strength

The candidate also needs people skills to enable a smooth transition in leadership and management styles between organizational cultures.

So which candidate profile is the best? It's not Roger. While Roger is a strong operator—one of the best performers at his level—he has not demonstrated his ability to operate at a more strategic level (at least as others rated him on this 360-degree survey). While this might not rule him out, the fact that he also has a shortfall on global mindset puts him at a disadvantage in the new role outside the United States. If his learning orientation were higher (also below the norm and his third development opportunity area overall), perhaps he would be able to build new skills and overcome some of these obstacles. But given this profile, the company would not choose Roger for such a strategic international assignment.

Victoria, on the other hand, excels in those very same areas where Roger has gaps. She has clear strengths in strategic thinking and a global mindset. She is also a strong and inspiring leader who collaborates extremely well. Would the company choose her for the role? Perhaps, but most likely not. Despite her five clear strengths, her shortcomings in the two areas of setting direction and operational savvy would be enough to halt her placement. Her company's concern about Victoria would be that, while she can energize people and think big thoughts, she might not be able to execute.

In the end, Joy, who has the fewest clear strengths overall at only two (operational savvy and learning orientation), is probably the best choice. She has a blend of capability in all the areas needed and is exceptional at both execution and learning. She will likely learn whatever else she needs to accomplish her goals. Her only glaring shortcoming is inspirational leadership, and that is probably more about style (given that a global mindset and collaborating in a matrix organization are solid) than bad behavior. Joy might even be someone who has been seen at times as being a solid B player instead of a superstar, but her consistency across the competencies and strengths needed are the right mix for the role. If the role had been more about setting the strategy (with execution being given to a different team or leader), then the choice would easily be Victoria.

Personality Tests

A personality test is another form of survey, but you are usually the only person filling it out. You probably have taken at least one if not several personality tests already, in school, as part of a team-building exercise, or in a hiring process. Perhaps you've even completed one of those simple twenty-item questionnaires in your favorite magazine about the type of person you are or what you prefer in a future partner. Personality tests are often used in assessments of potential. Although they can be based on many different theories and models, the field of psychology is aligned around one set of five "big factors" of personality (called the "Big Five") that span all types of models and measures: extraversion, agreeableness, conscientiousness, openness to experiences, and neuroticism.

While the field of psychology has settled in on the Big Five, the tests that organizations use in talent applications vary. Many on the market, such as the Hogan Personality Assessment Suite, report on more factors than just these five. No matter which tool is used, however, the measurement process is the same—all self-reporting. You fill out your own responses.

Advice for taking a personality test. The goal of the test is to help understand your general foundational tendencies and what drives you. Your company is also assessing whether you have developed ways to adapt to any potential challenges, based on your personality. For example, if you are an introvert yet want to work in a large company where relationships are vital, do you know how to overcome your introversion and have you done so in the past? Similarly, if you are naturally neurotic and high strung, do you always appear anxious at work? Or have you found a way to contain that energy and demonstrate a calming manner, as a senior leader probably should?

You may be thinking, why would I ever admit that I'm neurotic and high strung, among other things? Well, you're not directly answering questions about these internal states (at least, not in the more sophisticated measures used in assessment programs). Instead, a number of items typically load on scales of importance. There is no easy way to fake or game a personality test. Some tools have hidden indexes that tell the interpreters you tried to manipulate the outcome. So, you generally need to take the questions asked at face value. Do your best to follow the instructions when filling out the assessment, moving through the items as quickly as possible, and with a frame of reference toward work (and not personal life), unless the tool is telling you to do otherwise.

Do not take the assessment in multiple sittings, for example, when traveling between flights. It can skew your judgment and produce some startling and odd outcomes in the report, making interpretations in a talent review meeting next to impossible.

One executive attempted to complete his personality test during the course of a week when he was traveling extensively. He completed one segment in an airport lounge, the next section in his hotel room two nights later after a day full of meetings, and the third in the town car on the way home from the airport. The outcome was a pattern of results in which he appeared to be very excitable, prone to rash decision making, and easily rattled, while simultaneously having no anxiety, a high degree of impulse control, and strong judgment, and always calm and even tempered.

Taking and retaking personality tests is unlikely to help. First, many of the tools have been designed to detect this behavior with "faking indices" or tests for socially desirable answers. The result will be that your responses will be tagged as invalid, and everyone will know you tried to manipulate the results. Second, regardless of how much time passes between tests, your core personality assessments remain stable over time. While some changes can occur (and are more likely to as you get older and major events happen in your life), the results are usually pretty consistent.

One of us was working with a very senior leader who had just received his feedback on a personality tool. Although the results indicated he had a strong and charismatic leadership profile, he was less than happy about his middle-of-the-road scores on the dimension of inquisitiveness. He felt he was more creative and intellectually curious than the tool indicated. He suggested he had an "off" day the first time he was assessed and asked to retake the personality survey. He scored only slightly higher on "inquisitive," despite his clear interest in increasing it significantly the second time. His other scores on the assessment were almost identical. It wasn't all that easy to influence the scores, despite his clear awareness of what he wanted to change.

Interviews

Interviews are similar to 360-degree feedback in that they focus on behaviors and experiences you demonstrate in your workplace, only this time an interviewer is asking you questions directly. While some organizations use internal interviewers, in many assessment programs, outside parties are used to collect the data to raise the level of confidentiality. The downside, of course, is that the organizational culture and work context gets lost. External interviewers don't know about your extremely demanding business-to-business customer or the challenges of your work with your audit organization, and thus, the behavioral examples won't be as engaging as they might be to an internal assessor.

Interview data by its very nature is less quantitative, so it requires a content or theme analysis (see chapter 5 for more on how this is done) to turn into actionable information. When it conducts an interview for a talent management process, your organization focuses on measuring individual capabilities on the most critical competencies from its leadership framework. For example, if your organization is evaluating strategic thinking, questions the assessor might ask are: "Tell me about a time when you faced a significant business challenge that required you to develop a new strategic solution to solve it. What was the context of the challenge? What were the elements of your strategy? How did you develop your strategy? What happened as a result of implementing the strategy? What did you learn as a result of working on that challenge overall?" The assessor would have a scoring key or template with the types of examples to look for in determining how well you did on the interview.

How to prepare for an interview. You can positively affect interviews by listening carefully to what the interviewer is asking and then being clear and concise in your responses based on your experiences and learning. Try not to present yourself in a monotone voice without passion for your work, your people, the company, or your career. Body language matters here.

You can do a little more to prepare if you know about the interview process beforehand. Some organizations use the interview to determine competencies demonstrated in your past behaviors (called critical incidents). In these cases, before you attend an interview, review the leadership framework of your organization as well as your past work history and your résumé. Recall strong examples where you did your best (or where you learned the most from the situation). Make sure you are prepared to describe these illustrations articulately with sufficient detail about your career successes, challenges and adversity you have faced, tough relationships, biggest lessons, failures, and so on.

A scoring team is likely to break down your stories into content segments and code with ratings to have analyzable data for discussion at the talent review. For example, a reviewer might look at how you talked about your people and what you did for them during a case example of a major change effort. Did you demonstrate empathy and concern for their well-being or were you "all business" when implementing the latest produc-

SAMPLE BEHAVIORAL INTERVIEW TOPICS

- Tell me about a time when you had to lead a large organizational change project with complex issues and diverse stakeholder groups. How did you manage the different needs of the stakeholders? How did you go about engaging your stakeholders to build support and ensure implementation?

- Describe a situation when you struggled to build an effective working relationship with someone important. How did you eventually overcome this challenge (or did you)?

- Share with me an example of when you did not meet a client's expectation. What happened, and how did you attempt to solve the situation?

- Describe a time when you had to work closely with someone whose personality or leadership style was very different from yours. How did you address these differences?

- Give me an example of when you were able to successfully influence someone to see things your way—someone who may have been initially holding a different point of view or even was opposed to your perspective.

- Tell me about a time when you were able to be creative with your work. What was exciting or difficult about it? What made your approach creative versus other ways of addressing the work?

tivity effort (i.e., demonstrating head but no heart)? More sophisticated organizations have an interviewing team calibrate the ratings to make sure the depth of stories is equal across individuals.

Interviewers will probe for details, but they are unlikely to tell you directly what they want to hear or which behaviors they are asking about. So you need to identify great career experiences with many complex dynamics and discuss those as a starting point. The more insightful and thoughtful the story, the better the score. The sidebar "Sample Behavioral Interview Topics" contains sample questions often used in practice.

Cognitive Abilities Tests

Cognitive abilities tests are designed to measure various aspects of your verbal, numerical, spatial, problem solving and critical thinking skills. In short, they measure your aptitude to learn and process information. If you've ever taken a standardized test for school (such as the SAT, GRE, GMATs, etc.), you are likely quite familiar with some derivative of these tools. Because cognitive abilities tests are also associated with general measures of intelligence (IQ), however, they are probably one of the most intimidating types of assessments to take.

Cognitive abilities tests are used far more frequently for external selection of candidates than internal leadership development efforts. The reason is simple. It is very difficult (if not impossible) to change your level of cognitive skills. You might be able to develop work arounds or alternative strategies for solving complex problems, but general intelligence levels are thought to be fixed. Therefore, it is better to use these types of tools for selecting talent into your organization rather than developing people once they are inside already. That said, companies do employ certain types of cognitive tests aimed at problem solving and critical thinking skills to help improve the identification of high potentials among the talent pools they have internally. Church and Rotolo's benchmark research reported that almost 40% of their sample of eighty marquee companies use them today both with high potentials and senior executives. Some of the more commonly employed tools include the Watson Glaser Critical Thinking Appraisal, the Wonderlic, and the Ravens Advanced Progressive Matrices.

How to prepare for a cognitive abilities test. When it comes to preparing for cognitive abilities tests, there is not much you can do other than focus on the task at hand. As with many of the other assessments, be sure to get a good night's rest before taking the assessment and follow the instructions provided (often these tests will be timed or even proctored to minimize cheating). The best guidance we can give is to practice with sample items ahead of time. If you know what type of cognitive test is being used, it might help to review sample questions in advance (many can be found online). For example, Ravens is a nonverbal online test comprised of puzzles (some people enjoy these), whereas the Watson Glaser focuses on text-based comprehension assessment much like the GREs.

Testing for the Elusive "Executive Presence"

A recent study focusing on what companies use to identify potential noted that about 35 percent measure "executive presence" in some way.[6] While executive presence is neither an X factor nor a recognized personality trait or leadership competency, many companies use it in talent reviews when describing people. Yet no one can really tell you exactly what it is. If you ask senior leaders in almost any company, they will say they "know it when they see it." It is close to the concept of "potential," though they are not mutually exclusive.

In reality, executive presence is a combination of many different elements that can differ greatly from organization to organization. Sometimes it is simply the sum total of the qualities many executives in an organization share. Despite being difficult to define, executive presence is real to most senior leaders when they discuss an individual's talent. You need to understand what it means concretely in your organization and then consider how you might be perceived in this area.

For example, consider a brilliant programmer who has the smarts to lead an organization but lacks the polish to influence at senior levels. She may be missing the ability to be concise, often diving too deeply in her presentations on what executives end up considering tangents (i.e., she is limited in her skill at complexity translating). Or consider the buttoned-up executive who always looks the part, but many consider him to be an empty suit as soon as they discuss business strategy with him. He might go a certain distance because he is likable and polished in presenting, but eventually his lack of capability catches up with him. This usually results in an exit or termination because of the seniority he has achieved and the scale of his impact. One of the reasons organizations use assessment tools so much is that the resulting data can speed up the process of identifying both of these cases. Assessment tools can help the company work with the programmer to prepare her to advance, while at the same time showing the empty suit to the door.

Even if you can't figure out precisely how your bosses and their bosses define "executive presence," focusing on the five X factors will help you be perceived as possessing it.

How to Influence the Assessment Process

The assessment process can seem intimidating, but you can influence it in positive ways.

First, try to find out which tool or tools is the most important in influencing the talent review. Your organization and the leaders involved in making the talent decisions will determine which ones carry the greatest weight. Your company's culture, your managers' perspective on your future (and your potential), the type of roles being filled, and any biases for certain measures will influence the process. For example, your direct reports' perceptions from a 360-degree survey might be more important than your peers' or your boss's. In this case, it means that the executives making the selection are focused on core leadership and management skills and how you work with your team. Other organizations might emphasize your personality profile (are you a big-picture thinker and creative enough to lead the business forward?), or perhaps on the assessment center results (are you a natural collaborator and do you handle conflict well with your peers under stress?).

In general, a good way to determine what the organization values is what it spends a lot of money on. All assessment processes take time and cost money. So if you are being considered for a role and there is an assessment (or even if there a general assessment process that you nominate yourself for), consider the size and scale involved. That may well indicate its importance and how much weight it has in your review. For example, if the company is willing to invest a full day offsite for an assessment center with external industrial-organizational psychologists involved in the process, it probably counts a great deal.

Second, focus on the things that will help you do your best:

- Represent yourself honestly and accurately.

- Be prepared if pre-work is provided.

- Know what is important to the organization and brush up on your skills ahead of time if you will be assessed for content knowledge.

- Come fresh and ready to engage if interviews, assessment centers, or simulations are involved.

- Take the process seriously; devote time and space on your calendar if needed.

- Keep our X factors front and center at all times.

What to Do *After* the Assessment Process

One consistent insight we have gained from our experience is the positive influence or halo that some people receive from formally acknowledging their own developmental opportunities and having a detailed, thoughtful development plan in place. Organizations generally require that you develop these plans after attending or being part of an assessment program. Similarly, almost certainly following a talent review process or a leadership program, individuals seen with potential for larger roles will have plans the company puts in place to help them.

However, we have observed that those individuals who proactively work out a developmental agenda and share their insights and plans before the organization requires them to are more likely to be seen as stars. They recognize their own limitations (or at least some of them) and are working toward a solution through learning and growth. As we have discussed before, learning is a leading indicator of potential. Even if you focus on the wrong areas from a company point of view (e.g., you are deepening your consumer insights skills to be a better marketer when the organization wants you to develop your global mindset instead), the very act of focusing on your learning and growth as a leader matters.

Conversely, those individuals indifferent to their own development will eventually fall out of the high-potential designation. Many assessment measures such as the Hogan Personality Assessment Suite, interviews, and even some 360-degree feedback survey tools will pick up these tendencies. A weakness unrecognized, ignored, or just plain papered over by arrogance is not likely to play well in any talent review process. While you might have convinced your manager of your capabilities, others will have seen your shortcomings. This could be your downfall in the short (or long) run.

Gather your own feedback from colleagues or at least spend time reflecting on your own strengths and opportunities, and craft a serious plan for improving yourself. Think long term about the types of roles you would like in your present organization and what it might take to get to them. If your plan is focused on broadening out your experience set, identify the roles from which you could learn the most. Should you plan for a role in a different business sector or perhaps in another country? Do you need to try a different function to round out your skills or perhaps work in the corporate headquarters to better understand the corporate politics or enterprise strategy? Perhaps you need an experience in field operations instead or working with one of your largest customers. Or maybe you need to experience the thrill (and risks) of working on a new venture. If instead your plan is focused on developing or enhancing a specific set of skills such as inspirational leadership, think about what steps you might take in your current role to build this capability. Should you develop a manifesto with a clear vision for your team to rally behind? Engage an external coach or partner with someone internally who can observe you in action and give you real-time feedback? Or perhaps spend time building deeper relationships with each of your direct reports, getting to know their career interests and soliciting concrete ideas for enhancing your team's functioning?

In the end, there is no simple answer. The best path to development is one that will resonate with your needs and situation and one that you will personally commit to following through. If you can create your own version of a draft development plan that captures some of this content, you will show that you are thinking broadly about your talent and career aspirations in general. If you can capture all this and talk with your boss and others, you will help your quest for leadership success. At a minimum, others will know what you want, and you're very likely to learn what's standing in your way.

What Not to Do in High-Potential Talent Processes

One final area is what *not to do* in preparation for talent reviews and the high-potential process. First, be certain the information you provide is accurate and honest. Don't ever falsify anything in your background. In addition, don't use threats to leave your organization as a means to accelerate consideration for a high-potential designation. Both will backfire. (We'll say more about the consequences in chapter 8.)

Also, don't skip or delay an assessment. Participate even if you fear doing poorly. Assessments cost millions of dollars annually, so when a company identifies someone to go through a program, it is usually interested in investing in them for a reason. If your company has asked you to participate, do so enthusiastically. If you decline or try to put it off, you are sending a message, whether intentional or not, that you don't want to be a serious contender for the high-potential pool. Some organizations may give you one pass for business reasons and a second chance to participate; others are likely to write you off at that point. Either way, they will doubt your ability to take on more. After all, if you don't have confidence in your ability to do well, why should the company?

Don't expect (or ask for) time off to do the assessments (or have other priorities removed). High potentials are expected to find the time to complete assessments in addition to their day jobs, as yet another indicator of their ability to take on greater and more complex responsibilities.

. . .

The data generated from formal assessment tools is only one element a company uses in making a decision about your potential. The ultimate determination happens in a formal meeting when people discuss talent and make placement or promotion decisions. Thus, the most important organizational process influencing whether you are ultimately designated a high potential is called the talent review. Unless you have been in a talent review meeting, you probably have no idea how it works. For many, it represents another black box of HR.

In the next chapter, we will take a deeper look at the review, including another key component that you need to get right in advance—your employee profile, the one document that contains your critical information. Decision makers will rely on this source when discussing your future. Ensuring that your organization has the most accurate and up-to-date information is vital.

Summary Lessons

- If your company asks you to participate in a simulation, devote the appropriate amount of energy and focus. The more you know about the business, leadership, and cultural imperatives of your organization, the better off you'll be in the simulation.

- If a simulation involves other people, be on your best behavior even when stressed; this may be exactly what the assessors are testing you on.

- 360-degree feedback surveys are generally difficult to influence directly to improve your scores. While some people try to select only their friends and allies as raters, hoping for more favorable scores, this strategy can backfire. Many 360-degree survey processes include an oversight review to counter bias. Sometimes your friends feel the need to give you the most honest feedback. Ensure that you select a good range of individuals with whom you work closely on a regular basis.

- There is no easy way to fake or game a personality test. Many have hidden indexes that tell the interpreters you tried to manipulate the outcome. Take the questions at face value. Do your best to follow the instructions when filling out the assessment, moving through the items as quickly as possible and with a frame of reference toward work. Do not try to take these assessments in multiple sittings.

- If you are assessed in a behavioral interview and prompted to recall examples where you did your best, make certain you can convey them articulately with sufficient detail. Identify great career experiences with many complex dynamics, and discuss those as a starting point. Anticipate the most likely topics, identify your stories beforehand and think through the critical details you want to convey.

8

The Talent Review

Making Certain Your Organization Has a Clear Picture of Who You Are and What You Want

The next major hurdle you have to tackle is the organization's talent management process. Your manager and other leaders will come together to discuss people and determine who the high potentials are. Even if you are a fantastic performer and your boss loves you, you could well come out of this review with a "solid B player" label on your forehead instead of the high-potential designation you so keenly desire. In short, while knowing what it takes to get high-potential status and demonstrating the right behaviors every day, you must still find a way to navigate through what many have called "the black box" of the talent review process.

In this chapter, we are going to take you inside that black box to help you successfully jump this hurdle. We will describe what happens in reviews, as well as the components that are often included as part of the broader talent management system that supports it, including everything from the basic employee profile that is essentially your internal online résumé to the value of individual career development plans. While all the

HR forms, tools, assessments, and processes can be intimidating, they provide an objective view of your strengths and gaps, giving you and your organization insights into whether you are a good fit for a given job or even for your company.

What Really Goes On in Talent Reviews?

When people talk about the black box behind talent decisions, they mean primarily the talent review meeting. This formal meeting at which leaders get together and review their people takes place at least once but sometimes several times a year. General Electric put this process on the map with its review, "Session C." Other companies, such as PepsiCo, call it "People Planning."

Regardless of the name, you should see these reviews positively. Your organization needs a way to carefully review its talented people, identify those with the highest potential, and then decide on a slate of candidates who best fit upcoming job openings. The organization also needs a way to identify and debate who are the best and brightest. Who in the junior ranks has the potential to one day run the company? What needs to be done to help them develop quickly and effectively? Most talent processes are not much more complex than that.

Yet, a sense of mystery often surrounds this process, particularly if you don't know how it works or what's been said about you personally. After all, your bosses (or your boss's boss) head into a secret meeting. When the meeting is over, the information about how they made decisions is usually limited, but everyone knows that your future and that of your peers was the topic. Some colleagues are anointed or reaffirmed as high potentials. Others are simply designated as talented B players who the organization wants to keep. Sometimes even the C players are discussed.

Here, the situation sensing X factor is important because your best bet for success is to have your boss be a true advocate for you. You also want to ensure that you have made a highly positive impression on your boss's peers, other senior leaders, and of course, your HR professionals.

While organizations differ in the degree to which these meetings are formal or informal and what they cover (sometimes larger organizational issues such as structural changes, mergers, resources needed, organizational culture and employee engagement, or business trends are discussed as well), they all follow the same general pattern. There are three core components to every talent review:

- A presentation and discussion of individual employees (i.e., you), including your performance and career history, your work experiences, and your career aspirations and preferences, mobility constraints, and so on

- Some additional information, often informed by data from formal assessments, presentations in leadership programs, group sessions, interviews or other methods regarding your relative degree of strengths and opportunities and potential to take on broader roles

- A review of the organizational context in which current or future roles will be open for various reasons (e.g., other promotions, retirements, performance issues, new business ventures, new capabilities needed) to meet the needs of the business—roles that you might be considered for

Figure 8-1 shows a sample profile that includes some elements in an employee profile.

During the course of the talent review meeting, all bosses present an overview of their people, debating their merits and trajectory (i.e., career destination role), and weighing possible future jobs and types of work experiences that might best suit their reports' career goals and the business requirements. After everyone has reviewed and weighed in, the goal is to reach consensus (or at a minimum, alignment) on the individuals under review and the future assignment and development steps going forward. It's that simple (though the resolution of decisions in those meetings is not always easy). There is not a lot of magic behind this curtain. That said, these meetings are critical to determining whether or not you are a

FIGURE 8-1

Sample employee profile

Name: John Doe
Title: Director of Marketing
Business: Lucky Games
Location: Shanghai
Position: 1.3 years
Tenure: 3.5 years

Highest degree: MBA
School/univ: UCLA
Specialty area: Finance

Corporate experience:
- Senior Manager Marketing, US Action Figures
- Manager Marketing, US Educational Toys

Critical experiences gained:
- US experience
- Multi-portfolio
- Leading a large team
- Turnaround

Prior experience:
- Manager Marketing, Information Systems Engineer
- Associate Marketer, Educational / Technical Manuals

Critical experiences:
- International experience
- Different industries
- Startup

Career aspirations:
- CMO Lucky Corporation

Mobility: Anywhere Lucky operates
Languages: Fluent in English, Spanish

true high potential. They are also where many decisions about big promotions are made.

Now we'd like to tell you that your status as to whether you're a high potential receives a robust discussion every time, but this is not the case. The likelihood of an in-depth discussion of your capabilities depends on three factors:

1. Your level in the organization (the more senior you are, the more likely your future potential will be discussed in detail)

2. The degree of formality, rigor and time allocation that your organization's talent review process follows

3. The preparation and perceptions of your boss.

For example, your boss prepares for the meeting and presents his or her assessment of your potential to the group with whatever data and rationale that they deem appropriate (or as required by the process). That said, your best chance of being seen as a high potential by the broader organization is to have your boss present the case for you being a high potential upfront in the review. It is relatively rare for someone presented as a B player at the start to emerge as an A at the end of the review. On the other hand, even if you are rated as a high potential when your boss enters the meeting, it is quite common (about 10 to 20 percent of the time) that it will end with you having been knocked off the list due to questions or negative feedback that others may know or have heard about you.

Thus, you want your boss to present you in the absolute best light possible. If your boss doesn't know you well or has a poor opinion of your capabilities (or worse, doesn't even attend the meeting), you are unlikely to be positioned as or remain as a high potential for long. Even if others think you have great potential, your manager is your primary advocate in the room. This was our reason for beginning this book with the first X factor of situation sensing. Your relationship with your boss is pivotal to your designation. The only exception might be if you have had a track record of being a high potential (and also a high performer is a must) in the past and have senior sponsors who are particularly enthusiastic about your continued future potential.

How to Influence the Talent Review Process

How do you influence the talent review process itself? What's the best method for ensuring you are well represented during the discussion? Surveys and assessments measure your strategic thinking skills, your financial acumen, or the degree to which you collaborate with others. This part of your employee profile is hard to prepare for and influence.

You need to ensure that you are always performing on all cylinders. If you are not a high performer, you are unlikely to be seen as qualified for future leadership roles. So you have to achieve at levels that exceed expectations. In chapter 2, we identified the four opportunity zones where you can distinguish yourself. You also need to focus on demonstrating and mastering all of the X factors, as these are key indicators of potential (even though your organization may not have articulated them directly). There are several additional levers you need to pull when the timing is right. First, you want to be keenly aware of the content that the decision makers are discussing about you, the sources of data they are using to measure or assess your capabilities, the types of roles that they see for your future, and, of course, when the review meetings are held. Second, you want to be sure that everyone in the meetings knows what you really want from your long-term career.

When they know these meetings are scheduled, some high-potential candidates threaten to leave the company if they are not promoted or given what they want. While some organizations respond to this ploy, and although there are times when it can work, it tends to irritate senior leaders and senior HR professionals. It raises the question of commitment to the organization, and loyalty to the boss or other senior sponsors. It also sends a negative vibe to everyone else. Some companies and peers go to great lengths to get these threatening folks out the door by steering headhunters (external recruiters) their way in the hopes that they make good on their threat. While this can constitute a breach of the employment contract (read the fine print—some companies have you sign a statement every year as part of your compensation package or code of ethics statement that you will not enable the solicitation of employees by outside parties) in many corporations, it happens nonetheless.

Some high potentials who have threatened to leave if not promoted learn that they have painted themselves and the organization into a corner. They end up leaving because their organization did not respond well to their line in the sand. Even if promoted, the experience can be so negative that the individual ends up leaving anyway in a year or two.

So our bottom-line recommendation is, if you feel the need to leave an organization, be prepared to do so and pursue a legitimate course of action. Avoid workplace drama and idle threats. Focus on building your capability as a leader and what you need to do to get there.

Make Sure Your Employee Profile Is Accurate and Complete

Your organization has a file on you with your work history, where you went to school, what you majored in, and at an absolute minimum your performance history at the company. Make sure that this file reflects your most important career highlights and is accurate and complete.

Years ago, this was called a "personnel file." It literally sat in a manila folder in a filing cabinet somewhere in the HR department. Today, it is more often called an "employee profile" and is in an entirely electronic format in one of several linked HR or talent management systems. Your boss, your boss's boss, HR, and others who might be considering you for future roles can likely access the file. This data is not something secret or hidden, but a positive resource, a representation of you and your capabilities. Consider it your online résumé. It's like having an internal LinkedIn profile. This profile is used in talent review meetings in organizations of all shapes and sizes to facilitate the discussion of different individuals.

The good news is that this information is generally transparent and available to everyone with appropriate access to it. While different users have different levels of accessibility (e.g., your manager and HR can see everything while your direct reports and peers might be able to see only your educational background and work history but not your career aspirations or performance ratings), there is only one source of information on you as an employee. This also becomes important when your next boss wants to find out about who you are and what you've done. The first thing a potential new manager asks for when considering you for a role on her team is your profile.

The bad news is that, if this information is incomplete or inaccurate, you may not be represented favorably. Sometimes, people join companies and forget to enter their data initially. They get so busy that they never get around to updating their prior work experience or mobility preferences in the employee profile. So, when the time comes to review it for a promotion some two years later, the information is simply not there. Even if you did provide your information when you joined the company, it might be incomplete and out of date. And organizational changes and new technologies can have an impact on the quality of the data that exists.

For example, consider what happens to your data if you join a company that is later acquired by another much larger one and then, still later, merges with a third. You would hope that your information flows through each merger. Unfortunately, because companies use different HR data systems and need to harmonize to a single solution every time there is a major change, data can be lost. When your company is not on a major information technology platform that many other companies use, transfer is difficult. You might call this data "lost in translation," and it can affect any number of different data fields. While your name and title are probably correct, everything else is potentially at risk.

In some companies, we've seen prestigious high-potential leaders from a merged company who lost their all educational history in a data transfer (even their high-potential designations). That the data was missing was not noticed until the talent review meeting. Imagine having spent the time and hard work required to earn a Harvard MBA, only to learn that it was not in your profile, and the leaders in the review meeting assumed you had only a bachelor's degree. Or perhaps you and two peers are up for the same promotion to a director role in Latin America. You are the only one who speaks Spanish and Portuguese fluently, and you have prior work experience in the region as well, but all three of the profiles have no information in the language section or your work history and don't indicate that you should clearly be the one chosen. Or what if you spent five years before joining your current company running a branch office for a major retail chain. During this time, you had significant front-line managerial experience, yet at your present company, you only manage a few people. If your current bosses don't know about your previous work history, they might think you're not yet ready for a bigger role managing a large business unit.

So you need to ensure that the data in your profile is as complete as possible, accurate, and up-to-date. The first step is to check the systems you have access to and see your current information. In some situations, it will be easy to find on your home page or intranet, along with clear instructions for updating the information. In other cases, the profile might be harder to find or perhaps even hidden (or parts of it hidden) from your view. The best approach is to schedule a formal discussion with your boss about your career (as we discussed in chapter 2). During this conversation, ask to see your profile or background information so that you can ensure it is correct. If you have difficulty doing this, the next step is to meet with your HR professionals. Not only should they be able to give you a view of the information, but you might find that they are good listeners and career counselors as well.

In theory, keeping your data up-to-date should be simple. You should only need to update your background once and then check periodically (e.g., following a new job or promotion) to ensure that your new roles and performance ratings are captured. Some companies have specific times of the year when they encourage employees to go into the tools and update their data so take advantage of these as well. If the organization's HR information systems are working well, and your data is limited to just these simple areas, this might be the case. In some organizations, however, the HR systems are not advanced or automated, resulting in incomplete or inaccurate data. As we noted, when companies have grown through acquisitions or mergers, one HR system may not be connected to the other.

Profiles can capture much more about you than these simple elements. More sophisticated companies may have far richer descriptive information in your profile. Additional information might include work experience, mobility, career aspirations, internal and external advanced skill training, awards, and certifications.

Work experiences gained. While most companies capture the job titles in your past history, some go further and catalog the type of work and sometimes critical experiences you have had (for more, see the sample list in chapter 4 on career piloting). Classic research on high potentials in many different types of companies indicates that people learn from experiences more than anything else (e.g., task forces, special assignments, formal training, mentoring, coaching, etc.). So it is sometimes helpful to know what people have actually done in prior roles. Even knowing certain basic attributes of the experiences is useful in determining the breadth of your experiences. For example, a profile might note that you had two jobs titled "marketing manager" during a four-year window. If these two roles were in very different parts of the business in different geographies (e.g., one in a developed market such as the UK and one in an emerging market such as India), it would really say something different about you and how you performed in highly divergent conditions.

Another advantage of enhanced profile content is the depth of information about each experience. For example, your profile might indicate that you had outstanding performance in your prior job as the director of shipping, northeast region, from 2014 to 2016. But the title alone conveys nothing about what you did in the role, whether your performance was exceptional, or what you learned from the assignment. Instead, some information in your profile indicating that in your first operations role, you led a major and successful transformation of the shipping process is far more helpful. Or maybe you implemented a brand-new process, upgraded the performance by managing out (i.e., terminating) the bottom ten percent of performers, and did this all while delivering above-target results. That's the profile of someone who delivers results and has significant potential to do more in the future as well.

If your organization captures information about your experiences gained or offers the ability to provide details about your performance and lessons in prior roles, take advantage of it.

Mobility. Ensure that your profile indicates whether you are willing to move to another state, region, or country to take on a new role or promotion. Consider what happens if you say that you are mobile and your company suggests you for a role in a location you don't want to live in and you say no. Does that mean you will forgo a promotion and lose a shot at a high-potential designation in the future? The answers to these questions all depend on the company, the roles available, and you. But the bottom line is that mobility still matters to organizations, and your profile needs to be clear about your intentions. Remember, the employee profile is the key source of information used to describe you holistically in the talent review meetings.

In the last forty to fifty years, organizations have shifted their thinking about how to manage the mobility of their workforces. In the 1960–2000s, many companies had the idea that everyone should be willing to move to wherever needed. It was called a "tap on the shoulder." One day, you were leading a team in Boston, and the next day, you were told to pack up and move to Shanghai. Today, however, the dynamics are different due to changes in the employment contract, new generations of workers, increasing numbers of dual-career couples and families, and extended elder-care situations. Organizations know they cannot simply tell people when and where they need to go for a new job or promotion. In response, their employees will simply turn them down or leave.

From one perspective, the organization still needs to staff with the best possible talent in every market, whether in New York, Los Angeles, Mexico City, Dubai, China, or the UK. This is why having information about your mobility in talent reviews is so important. While companies often emphasize staffing with local talent (for a number of reasons, including knowledge of the culture and cost savings), some prime roles are held for high potentials to cycle through in order to learn different aspects of the business in various parts of the world. But to plan for this effectively, organizations have to know who is willing to move, so the accuracy of the employee profile once again becomes important.

Organizations differ in how much detail they capture here, but they are interested in knowing where you want to go and when. Ensure your organization knows your interests and willingness to live in the different locations in which it operates. Your expressed willingness and interest to relocate becomes a major component in the planning discussed at talent review meetings. If you can't move from a particular location to help grow the business, you may limit your career opportunities, even if everyone agrees that you are high-potential talent.

Career aspirations. Similar to profile information about mobility, many organizations also track information regarding your expressed career goals and aspirations. While the more sophisticated talent systems and processes might contain detailed career plans with destination roles in mind (e.g., "we see you as becoming the CFO one day and here is the plan to get there"), even the most basic talent review discussions often include the question, "What does she want to do with her career?"

We reiterate the importance of having career conversations with your boss. These conversations will resurface in the review meetings. Your boss may or may not be in the room during a talent review meeting. If you have career aspirations and goals that you have not clearly articulated and as a result are not added to your profile, your company might not consider you for certain types of opportunities. It needs to know you want to get promoted. If you were offered that sales leader job in North Carolina tomorrow, would you pack up and take it? It also needs to know your long-term goals. Do you want to be a CFO one day and therefore have a deep functional career in finance? Or are you really interested in being more of a general manager and are open to trying out more lateral roles in other functions such operations, sales, marketing, or even HR to develop a wider set of skills for the long haul? As we noted earlier, however, you must not be insistent about the roles to which you aspire.

Of course, do not falsify any profile information about your background (e.g., lying about your educational degree or institution or former employment history) or internal experience. This is not only wrong but could have legal consequences. We have seen people claiming to have MBAs from prestigious universities when they do not. If you have a degree and it's not listed in your profile, make sure it is there. But if you don't have one, don't make it up. Sooner or later, someone will find out. The higher you go, the bigger the risk to you and the company. Just don't do it.

Make Sure Your Interests Are Known

Making sure your file is complete and accurate is the first step in influencing the talent review process. The other important factor within your control is ensuring that your interests are clearly known and by whom.

First, determine who will be in the talent review meeting and that at least one or more of those individuals knows what you want and hopefully is an advocate for you and supports your interests in that area. If your boss is participating in the meeting, make sure you have had that conversation and have been very clear about your aspirations and preferences. If not (and sometimes even if they are going to be there), you may want to have had discussions with your boss's boss and your HR professional. Other peers of your boss (particularly if they are also mentors) can also be your advocates, particularly if their perspectives are consistent with yours.

For example, a manager interested in taking a new job outside the United States has "wired" her interests using a variety of means, including conversations with her immediate boss, her boss's boss, the boss she might be transferred to or promoted to be under, the HR professional, and possibly the HR professional in the part of the business she might be transferred to. By the time they all discuss this manager in the review meeting, everyone in the room knows what she wants to do next. Of course, this doesn't guarantee she will get the job, as others might ultimately be a better fit. But the manager's extensive conversations with all involved can certainly help as long as not seen as being underhanded or manipulating.

By having career conversations with your boss, HR, and others, you may learn that your aspirations are unrealistic or otherwise not aligned with the organization's perceptions of you. Even if you are a superstar high potential, the company may not see you as being able to stretch to fill the exact role you have in mind, but instead something equally as good. It's great to have aspirations (and high potentials are expected to have them), but if you are an operations professional who wants to be the chief legal counsel one day and don't have a law degree, you'll be seen as stretching too far. We've literally seen the opposite, that is, a senior legal professional with aspirations of being a country unit general manager, yet with no background in finance, supply chain, marketing, sales, or any other function remotely linked to running a business. While this might work in some companies, many would consider it too much of a reach without some developmental work to close critical gaps in knowledge and experience. Someone high in catalytic learning might get there, but it would still take a lot of effort.

Even the more subtle distinctions in how your organization currently sees you (and this can change) are worth exploring. Let's say you are in the finance function and want to be a country general manager, but the company sees you instead as a future CFO. You need to know this so you can make the right decisions for your future. Use your career meetings with others to find out. You don't want to appear overly ambitious for a promotion. Your bosses will take that as a sign you are shallow and not focused on the big picture of leadership or, at the very least, lacking in self-awareness. Either interpretation can harm your credibility and have an impact on your future opportunities. If you truly want to become the next CEO, but your organization doesn't see you in that position, then you and the organization need to make some thoughtful decisions about realistic aspirations.

Be Proactive

Your organization must have the most up-to-date information about you, including basic background information, interests, experiences, preferences, and aspirations at any given moment in time. If you can, update your profile frequently. When one element has not been updated in a profile, it throws into question the quality and timeliness of the data in the systems and on the entire form. Often, executives in the review meeting will disregard the whole form and wait for it to be completely fixed before going further with a candidate. You do not want this to happen during a decision-making window. In the end, your profile is a database representation of you. If you want to be a high potential, the organization needs to know as much as it can about you.

. . .

There is one final organizational element to consider before charging ahead with your high-potential goals. It's the focus of our next chapter, the cultural context of your organization. Just as catalytic learning is a foundational aspect of the other four X factors, the corporate culture where you work is foundational for all high-potential data, processes, and talent decisions. It provides an important overlay that influences the parameters and boundaries of how you attain high-potential status.

Summary Lessons

- Along with your performance record, your relationship with your boss is pivotal to what your designation will be in the talent review meeting. Ensure he or she is your advocate. Make certain you have periodic career conversations with your boss, sharing your aspirations and soliciting feedback on your career.

- Make certain you exceed performance expectations and focus on the four opportunity zones described in chapter 2. This is the baseline requirement in the review.

- Demonstrate and master to the best of your abilities all of the X factors, as these are key indicators of potential, along with any specific leadership competencies that your organization measures and rewards.

- For the talent reviews, you must ensure your organization has the most up-to-date information about you, including basic background information, interests, experiences, preferences, and aspirations, at any given moment. Keep it updated.

- Do not falsify any information about your background or internal experience.

9

Corporate Culture

Understanding the Forces That Shape People's Perception of You

Let's say you have embraced and excelled at all five of the X factors that differentiate high potentials from everyone else. Does your accomplishment automatically guarantee you a high-potential designation? Will the X factors help you to safeguard your status no matter how and where you move in your organization? Does the designation mean you'll be seen as a high potential if you move to another organization? The answer to these questions is, unfortunately, no.

While your true potential is something you will always have, your status as a high potential is enhanced or constrained by the corporate culture where you work. For this reason, you need to have absolute clarity about your organization's cultural demands. You must be willing to behave according to those demands. In many organizations, the senior-most leaders are even called *culture carriers*. They not only have to embody the best of the culture, but they have to reinforce and amplify critical norms in their decisions and actions. As your high-potential status takes you higher, you have to role model the "right stuff."

Since culture is the collection of values, norms, policies, and practices (both formal and informal) that influence the day-to-day life in companies, it profoundly shapes the ways in which individuals are evaluated in terms of their potential. Its power comes from the fact that it is the sum total of everything that the organization has learned about coping successfully with external challenges and organizing itself internally to match these external demands. For example, in one organization, relationships are of paramount value. The company's history has taught it the necessity of collaboration and teamwork. Early successes were built around project work that required different functions to work together in non-competitive and highly integrative ways. In another organization, winning as an individual is more highly valued. Its early successes were built around individuals championing a new product idea and in turn being highly rewarded *as individuals* for its success. Its internally competitive culture helped it exceed sales targets every year for the last fifteen years. While these two cultures are strong contrasts, each works to ensure its own success. The questions then are: In which one would you flourish given your disposition and talents? Do you prefer to work in collaborative teams or stand out as an individual performer?

As a consequence, what it takes to be perceived as a model citizen in one organization may not be at all the same in another. In most companies, what is valued by the culture can be just as important, if not more so, than our X factors. The identical behavior in one culture—say, starting meetings with small talk inquiring about weekend activities or family—might be seen as a positive way of warming people up. In another culture, it could be perceived as a waste of time and the mark of an unproductive or undisciplined manager. Without embodying the appropriate cultural imperatives in your behavior, you could be knocked out of a high-potential designation completely.

So you need to find ways to identify, understand, and adapt to the dominant cultural elements in your day-to-day behaviors and choices. If the fit between your own values and behaviors and your organization's cultural requirements are spot on, you'll feel very comfortable forging ahead with a brilliant career there. Sometimes, however, just uncovering the core cultural demands may be enough to make you question whether you are in the right organization in the first place. After all, to paraphrase from Milton's *Paradise Lost*, is it "better to rule in hell than serve in heaven"? You may come to realize that the cultural demands are far outside the bounds of who you are or want to be. We have seen this happen particularly when people decide to change companies and even industries. They underestimate the importance of "cultural fit" to their success as they make the leap to a new firm. If you stay within an industry, you'll learn the cultural styles of the key industry players simply by word-of-mouth descriptions and through comments on popular social media feedback sites like Glassdoor. But if you jump from, say, financial services to consulting, health care, or social services, you could be quite surprised at the radical differences between cultures.

You have to understand the culturally determined behaviors and actions that support or detract from perceptions of high-potential talent designations. These can define your career and whether you wish to remain or move on from your current organization. You have to gain these insights as soon as you step into your new organization. You'll face culturally determined tests in your very first meeting on the first day of your new job. You'll want to make the right choices in how you respond and engage with others. For instance, imagine that first meeting. You barely know the individuals around the table, not to mention the rules of the game. To whom do you need to be most responsive and how? Is it the person who has the highest position? Is it the individual who is the most active contributor? Or is it the folks from a particular function (e.g. finance or sales)? Should you be watching more closely the reactions of your team members or those from other teams? Should you debate a recommendation, support it, ask a series of questions, or just keep quiet as the new person? How should you respond when a senior leader turns to ask you a question point blank? To whom and to what you attend to matters when it comes to culture, and you need to figure it all out very quickly.

In this chapter, we will examine just how culture amplifies what it takes to be a high potential. We will also explore how culture determines your career path within the organization. From there, we will help you understand and read the most common cultural dimensions that you need to understand and act upon. And since culture matters from your very first day in a company, we will show you how to successfully learn about the culture and answer the critical question: "Am I a good fit here?"

Culture as an Amplifier or Derailer of Your High-Potential Status

How do the elements of an organization's culture affect whether you will be seen as a high potential or just another average hard worker? Ideally, culture would have no impact at all. "Potential" should be just that, your ability to succeed at higher levels. In reality, culture has either an amplifying effect or a derailing effect on your potential. And here's where it gets complicated: The exact same behavior, in two different organizations, could be either an amplifier or a derailer.

Take the example of an organization where people make final decisions off-line, in other words, *before* (pre-wiring) or *after* (closing the loop) the seemingly formal decision-making meetings. In these contexts, being a good situation sensor will only make you that much more successful. You'll know in advance that you need to connect with the three or four critical decision makers in a truly meaningful way by adapting your request or initiative to meet their needs. Assume that this small group will informally make the ultimate decisions related to your initiatives. If you master the legwork or "wiring" required to have decisions made in your favor, senior executives—including your boss and your boss's boss—will see you as the go-to individual who can get things done. They will come to rely on you to ensure that all the groundwork is laid with the right people. The more networked you are into the real informal decision process, the better able you will be able to navigate the political environment.

While this may sound straightforward, not every organization values decision making in this manner. In some cultures, pre-wiring decisions is considered counter to having a healthy, open, and honest discussion. These types of organizations believe that innovation and creativity are stifled when people work deals around the edges or through back-office politics. They frown heavily on managers who work that way. We've seen instances of high potentials caught working the back room, only to be called out as manipulative, deceitful, and dishonest. This is ironically the potential downside of being too good at situation sensing where it becomes an overused strength and ultimately derails your career in the wrong context.

The trick is figuring out just how the decision-making process works in your organization—when, how, and where it is appropriate to influence others. Then use your situation sensor skills to navigate accordingly. We'll show you how to make these assessments in this chapter.

Culture Profoundly Influences Your Career Destinations

Another way to think about culture and its impact on you is in terms of where your high-potential designation will ultimately take you. In some organizations, the high-potential designation is a broad concept (e.g., "she's a superstar, she has real potential."), and your career journey may end up highly opportunistic and remarkably unplanned—the herky-jerky kind. In others, it is about answering the question "potential for what end"? Are you a high-potential general manager, finance senior vice president, president of a business unit, or chief information officer? The concept of potential varies because organizations have different cultural beliefs and frameworks in place regarding the right way to build their senior leaders. For example, some companies place far greater emphasis on building breadth in the leaders at the expense of developing deep expertise, and others prefer to cultivate a deeper knowledge base in their senior leaders (e.g., where future technology or advances in science might be a key enabler of the business). In addition, organizations vary in the formality with which they engage in their talent development programs as well. Some have formal processes with clear career paths for progression, and others take a more organic approach that emphasizes the needs of the business over stability of structure. While there is no one best way to maximize your chances of becoming a high potential, you need to know how the organization thinks about senior leadership capability building and the pathways to get there.

Early in your career, organizations with more structured pathways upward can make a profound difference in where you end up decades later. For example, in many cultures, two and sometimes three functions are the high-status ones. In one organization, the most predictable pathways to the executive suite are through the finance and operations functions. In another, it will be sales and engineering. In another, global experience is critical for entering the executive suite.

Look around your organization and ask yourself: "What functions appear to produce the greatest number of high potentials?" "Do certain functional or other experiences appear to be critical stepping-stones to the executive suite?" If you are someone with a real passion for marketing and envision yourself as the chief marketing officer of a major social media or internet software company, you'll want to consider carefully whether to join any firm where these marketing backgrounds are largely absent among its executives. Instead, find the organization with strong brands where the CEO or several executives have impressive and relevant marketing experience.

Bottom line, you need to carefully assess the career paths of the senior team of the organization you are joining, and particularly the recent promotions, in case there is a new trend emerging. A critical dimension of an organization's culture is what functions are accorded the greatest influence. You can easily access all this information online if the firm is a publicly traded company. Even if it is privately held, most companies post the backgrounds of their executives on their websites.

A byproduct of these fixed functional pathways to the top is that certain skills and sources of knowledge become paramount for you to master early in your career. For example, Moheet Nagrath, former Chief Human

Resources Officer at Procter & Gamble, shared with us the imperative of persuasive writing skills (tied to our X factor of complexity translating) as a cultural demand for those wishing to ascend the ranks:

> During their early career, managers receive a great deal of coaching on how to communicate effectively—in writing and during presentations. There's an emphasis on writing concisely and persuasively—especially around one page memos which force the prioritization of what messages must be delivered. The purpose is to help individuals think rigorously through a proposal or a recommendation using a logical and succinct approach. The better thinkers become the better writers and stronger presenters. Not everyone gets to be good at this. In marketing—a critical function at P&G—it is a particularly important skill. Because this is a marketing-driven company, where advertising is the preferred way to convince consumers to try products, marketers have to be adept at persuasion. In addition to performance, these skills of communicating clearly and convincingly start to differentiate high potentials at the brand manager level. The importance of being able to write and present with skill becomes more pronounced as individuals move to higher levels of responsibility. They have to show that they can think clearly, decisively and analytically. To be clear, we don't say these skills automatically designate anyone as a high potential, but they are important contributors given what the culture values. As a result, most of the leaders in the company are powerful communicators in addition to their other leadership strengths.

Interestingly, this is an example of P&G's culture shining through in the way in which it communicates. In other organizations, for example, where leaders communicate entirely through PowerPoint presentations, writing memos might be completely foreign to them. In these cultures, the skill to learn quickly is how to communicate in the "house" presentation style (e.g., is it formal, informal, flashy, pithy?). Look around to see how presentations are structured, and how the discussions are managed (e.g., do people work from documents or presentation decks? Are they taking notes or using pen and paper, laptops or tablets?). But there are many ways to read a company's culture. There are signs to look for and dead giveaways to help you identify, understand, and adapt to the culture of your organization. We turn to this topic next.

Reading a Company's Culture: What to Look For and What to Embody

So how can you detect the essential elements of your company's culture? We begin with the arenas where cultural forces play out with the greatest variability with respect to their influence on your ability to be seen as a high potential. These big categories most typically define a company's culture. If you don't "match" on these elements, it will be hard for your colleagues to see you as a high potential, no matter your performance. Later, we dive more deeply into the two defining elements of culture—task indicators and social dynamics—and their implications for earning your high-potential designation.

Cultural Variables That Most Profoundly Shape Perceptions of You

At their core, organizations are simply large collections of people working together in structured or semi-structured ways to complete a common set of integrated tasks. Beyond formal structures and rewards, culture is the ultimate force that determines the concrete ways in which you personally engage in these tasks with your colleagues every day. Five arenas of culture are particularly relevant to high potential designations—relationships, communications, decision-making styles, individual versus group perspectives, and orientations to change. We'll discuss each next.

Relationships. While how you relate to and work with others matters in every company (and every organization says "relationships are important here"), what you need to determine is *how relationships are used to make decisions and coordinate actions*. How do people form and maintain relationships? Who is expected (even allowed) to initiate and what is expected as part of the exchange? For example—for a major decision, is one meet-and-greet with peers or superiors enough or do you need to have lunch or coffee weekly or monthly in order to influence decision-making? In some companies, the only way to have influence is to spend time with your coworkers for several days to bond. After that, calls or emails are fine. In other companies, video or conference calls are adequate for establishing relationships.

Communications. How do people in the company prefer to communicate with one another? Is the process always formal, with meetings scheduled beforehand, or can you simply pick up the phone or drop by someone's desk? In some companies, for example, you might never schedule a meeting with someone of a higher level to be held in *your* office. You would go to *their* office. Other organizations, however, use shared meeting spaces or informal areas for these types of meetings. What are the norms for information to be presented in meetings? Are presenters well prepared with slides? Are white papers or briefing documents the norm? Do leaders prefer preliminary reports so people come prepared or will they not read them anyway? Some organizations prefer fifty-page presentations with reams of details and analyses; others limit the discussion to a single page or no paper at all.

Decision-making styles. Does the culture have a bias for action or a bias for analysis and consensus? In organizations with a bias for action, people's time and attention spans are more limited, which significantly affects communications (e.g., providing key stakeholders with the information they need in advance so they can make a decision at the meeting).

Other companies prefer a more protracted discussion of options, models, and strategies, usually accompanied by large amount of supporting materials and analyses; as a result, people need more patience. The question here becomes, what is your own bias for action and does it fit perfectly with the culture? Would you enjoy the intellectual debate and consensus-building process or would it drive you nuts to spend so much time in discussions? Are you more the type who'd rather just decide quickly and move forward? The speed of decision-making may also translate to how the organization thinks about people and manages their assignments and promotions. So be sure to understand this going into a new company, so you appropriately align your expectations.

Individual versus group perspectives. Some companies approach work or jobs and their output as largely *the product of individuals*, while others focus their energies on *collaboration*. This approach is typically visible in how the company distributes performance rewards, but it can also be seen in internal competitive dynamics and/or branding differences between organizational units or businesses. If the organization is very individualistic in its approach, it will generally support a hero mentality, rewarding and recognizing the ambitious high potential. Unfortunately, this also increases the chance that the high potential will fall from grace (we call this going from "Hipo to Alpo"). Group-focused organizations provide more of a safety net, but they also make it harder for individuals to differentiate themselves. Once again, the key here is in how the company rewards and recognizes people, and what works best for you.

Orientation to change. The last cultural arena that can have an impact on your high-potential status is the organization's cultural orientation toward change management. In many cases, as a high potential, you are placed in situations where you are asked to drive change. As a matter of fact, you are likely to have many change-agent assignments in your career. By default, people have a natural and significant resistance (and a negative attitude) toward an incoming high-potential leader who is deployed to "shake things up." In organizations where change, however, is frequent and well accepted, change assignments are far less risky to your future career success (assuming you complete the goals of the assignment) than in those organizations where change is slow, often met with constant resistance, and rarely successful. These differences explain why internal star talents who are willing to challenge the conventions of their organization can either become high potentials or else completely derail their career.

The cultural orientation to change agents is simply an additional complicating factor here, and one you need to be highly aware of. If high potentials are brought in from outside the organization or promoted from the middle to executive levels, they've typically been told to shake things up by challenging the status quo. Unfortunately, many fail. They don't receive the proper onboarding (if any) or don't have the sponsorship of the senior leaders, and significant organizational resistance emerges. They end up not understanding that they have to play within the bounds of the culture. Many who derail mistakenly believe they have carte blanche to shake things up and ignore the culture. The challenge for any incoming (or internal) high-potential leader who is managing change is to determine what to challenge in the culture and what to honor and reinforce.

. . .

For a more precise understanding of where to adapt to cultural demands, we turn to task indicators and social dynamics. Observe which cultural conditions resonate the most with you. You'll end up with a much better sense of the types of organizations where you are likely to flourish and, in turn, become a high potential.

Task Indicators: How Work Gets Done

Task indicators are elements of culture that reflect *the ways in which work is accomplished*. These are the rules that people follow for how work is assigned and managed; how performance is measured; whether individual or team contributions are more highly rewarded; and the preferred approaches to performance deliverables and imperatives for compliance, safety, quality, and other standards. These indicators reflect the blocking and tackling of everyday work (e.g., the core tasks we described in chapter 2). While some may be codified in formal policies and programs, others are not. The sooner you figure out these indicators, however, the better off you'll be.

Some organizations expect that everyone has a particular set of metrics assigned to his or her role and needs to deliver against these metrics or goals in order to be rewarded. This is often the case in companies based largely on business models where generating high-volume outputs, such as sales, is key. Think about a car dealership where the number of cars you sell is literally the mark of performance success. There might be a team effort at the dealership level (and perhaps a bonus), but in the end, your pay and your future potential are based on your performance as an individual sales leader on the floor. If you don't sell enough cars, it doesn't matter how good a collaborator you are, even if you are beloved for organizing the company's softball games.

Individualistic cultures generally reward hero behavior over group achievement. In these environments, you must not only achieve all of the objectives articulated in your plan, but also overachieve on some or most of them. Your accomplishment can be at the expense of others (e.g., peers or colleagues) without it penalizing your career. In such competitive environments, the model is "winner takes all," making ongoing collaboration with peers difficult.

Other organizations, however, such as those in aerospace, pharmaceutical, or energy industries, have long lead times between the development of products and their commercialization. To bring their products ultimately to market requires a great deal of integration between functions. While individual achievements can still stand out in these environments, the cross-functional groups working on the project or delivering the service are more likely to be recognized as whole teams. As such, the culture rewards collaborative behavior and frowns on those individuals who try to stand out on their own. To be a high potential in this context, you may need to temper your ambition and focus more on your relationship skills, rather than highlighting your own unique contributions.

We list some additional task indicators of culture next. While not all have a direct bearing on your status as a high potential, knowing which ones represent hard lines in the sand for your organization is very important for your success.

Formal versus organic approaches to defining "work." One area in which organizations differ dramatically is in their level of formality in defining individual accountabilities and working relationships. Many companies, typically large ones with a deep history and culture, emphasize having clear job descriptions with very formal accountabilities. In these firms, you can usually find out the expectations of a given role, the reporting structure, and its relationships with other stakeholders (e.g., peers, customers, other functions, or parts of the business).

These organizations are a great fit for you if you like clarity about each. When your boss approaches you about taking a new job in these contexts, you can easily ask for the objectives and metrics. Clear accountabilities give an overall sense of clarity and stability to the day-to-day delivery of work and the longer-term career planning process.

Other organizations, however, have a much more informal culture with respect to jobs and roles. You might never know the expectations of a given role until you are sitting in it. In these more "organic" and often entrepreneurial organizations, reporting lines can be blurry or diffuse, and navigating them can be more challenging. Matrix organizations, where you might have more than one boss (e.g., a line of business and a functional leader), can further complicate the situation. But for some people, these are more fun as well. It all depends on your tolerance for ambiguity, as we discussed in the chapter on career piloting (see chapter 4). When considering a promotion in one of these companies, you are almost always walking into something new. People who are highly creative and entrepreneurially minded (e.g., high in our catalytic learning X factor) often choose more loosely structured roles in companies that follow this approach. The culture fits their need to go with the flow. If your ambitions, however, require you to see a clear path with known stepping-stones, the more formal organization is a better choice for you.

Decisions framed around critical stakeholders. In certain cultures, major decisions are made with a certain stakeholder always in mind. For example, if you are taking a role to work closely with a major customer organization, you might have to physically relocate to live and work near its headquarters for a few years during that assignment. This is quite common when working for consulting firms when junior professionals are stationed to work at a location in the client's organization. We've seen people who were sent to glamorous locations like Bermuda, Geneva, or Dubai. Others were sent to Detroit, Liverpool, or Tijuana. Of course, what is standard to one person might be glamorous and highly desirable to another, but either way, you need to be ready for it.

In other situations, the stakeholder consideration might be a real or perceived cost benefit. In one well-known hotel brand company, for example, the interests of property owners dominate most decisions. In another, an insurance company, the policyholders are always foremost. For example, a talented senior officer was being considered for an executive promotion. He had asked for special travel compensation if he took the job, because he did not want to move his family from their current location. His solution was to fly to the company headquarters to work during the week. He wanted the company to pay for his weekly airfare. One decision maker asked, "How will our policyholders benefit from flying this executive weekly to headquarters?" The answer came back from the executive decision makers reviewing his potential promotion that the company would not see enough benefit for the price, so it revoked the offer. Figure out who your dominant stakeholder group is and how to always integrate its perspective into your decisions.

Expectations for working with others. Another distinguishing cultural indicator is how people are expected to work with one another in such areas as meeting protocols, rewards and recognition, and ad hoc versus more structured approaches to teams. This often has nothing to do with size of the organization, but instead is the tone the senior-most leaders of the organization set. It has a trickle-down cultural effect on relationships. In one company we know, you are expected to give your full attention in meetings and actively contribute. In another organization, you can check your phone or laptop for urgent requests while in meetings. In both, these rules are in effect no matter what level or what function. They are symptomatic of deeper beliefs about how work is best done, either collaboratively where everyone involved or independently, with everyone striving to achieve their own personal best.

In companies where leaders are more open, approachable, and flexible, the ways in which others approach meetings, project planning, time-lines, contracting, and even staffing teams tend to be relationship based. You are more likely to be included in meetings with senior leaders than excluded. You are also more likely to be recognized for your contributions to the team's outcomes than your individual achievements.

While this may sound inviting at first—and it is for many people—it also means you focus more on relationship building, networking, and engaging with others than just on the tasks at hand. If you are an intro-vert and prefer heads-down intellectual work on your own, this can be intimidating. You will also likely need to do more to stand out as a high potential. For some leaders, particularly those who are traditional type A drivers, the dual focus on relationships and execution can be a big bar-rier to success. They tend to see the relationship-building demands as a waste of their time and so don't make sufficient investments. If you are also someone who wants to stand out and be recognized—for example, have your formal presentation on the agenda and be recognized for it—you'll want to seek out organizations that are more individualistic in their culture.

Questions to ask when determining this aspect of culture are: What is the company's approach to performance rewards? Does it have a pay-for-performance philosophy? Does it reward individual contributions or shared team contributions or are they weighted equally? Does it place a premium on and incentivize (e.g., via merit increases and annual bonuses) short-term contributions that are easier to make on your own, or is there a balance of short- and long-term incentives (e.g., via stock options, restricted stock units, or multiyear bonus payouts) that require a more strategic and collaborative approach? If so, what metrics or behaviors are these based on? How do people interact with each other on teams? Are they simply cordial or truly collaborative? Do outsiders typically stumble because they fail to build relationships first?

Social Dynamics: How People Are Expected to Interact with Each Other

The other major element of organizational culture is social dynamics, the ways people interact with one another informally. They reflect the broad range of unwritten rules for how to work with your colleagues. These relational rules of culture can make or break whether you are seen as a high potential.

Take the example of Scott, a high-potential software engineer who joined a manufacturing firm about ten years out of school. He has a strong résumé and great depth in his area of expertise. During the first six months in his new company, he quickly impressed his boss and other senior leaders with his innovative thinking and critical analyses of what the organization needed to tackle. He offered up a number of new process solutions that were compelling to several executives. So within his first year, Scott had been identified as a high-potential leader. As a result, he was given the reins on a number of key projects for the corporation, including leadership of a major software redesign of a core production system.

Despite knowing that the culture was somewhat resistant to outsiders and that relationships were of paramount importance, he chose to adopt a direct and focused style of project management. With executive support for his mandate, he felt a strong sense of urgency and believed that relationship building could wait until he had had some initial successes. He reassured himself that senior leaders appreciated his laser focus as a change agent and found his sense of urgency a breath of fresh air.

But within a few months, Scott's failure to invest up front in building constructive relationships with colleagues became his undoing. He had clues soon into the role, but he chose to ignore them. For example, early on, he observed that while his recommendations were greeted with positive nods of approval, they seemed to translate very slowly into actions. Soon after, he started to feel that people greeted his recommendations with more animated questioning about their feasibility. Finally, they met his proposals with a "thanks for the suggestion, but we've solved it ourselves already."

While his recommendations were likely sound, Scott had failed to build the network of relationships needed to implement them. His colleagues resented his failure to invest in them. In the end, Scott was downgraded from high-potential status to a key player. He was moved laterally to another position with far less impact, and twelve months later, he departed the company. Today, he is the head of his function in his current organization, where he fortunately found a stronger cultural fit.

The following questions address the social dynamics you need to detect and then model.

When and how is it is appropriate to reach out for help? For example, in some cultures, soliciting help from others is seen as a positive sign of openness and learning, a willingness to seek information and feedback, and a collaborative nature. In others, asking for help is an immediate indicator to superiors (and even worse your peers) that you are incapable of doing your current job, let alone having the potential for larger roles. In individualistic, task-oriented cultures, "helping" others perform their roles can lead to negative perceptions on everyone's part (even you, if you've helped someone else).

What constitutes going above and beyond the expectations of your job? Is success at all levels (i.e., poor, solid, great, superior) clearly defined within your performance goals? Or is the norm that you must do additional work beyond what you formally agreed to in order to be seen as a high potential? What do people really expect from others (peers, direct reports, and bosses) who are supposed to be high potentials? How are expectations measured? Are you recognized and appreciated for performing the primary responsibilities of your job or are you only recognized when you perform above and beyond what is required?

When should you challenge your boss, other superiors, and peers in meetings? This will vary according to your boss's interests, of course (see chapter 2), but the cultural overlay may be strong here as well. In some

organizations, bosses want to see your ability to debate ideas (in a respect-
ful way) in order to determine whether you have the analytical horsepower
and confidence that it takes to be a future leader. You need to know if
there are specific situations where you actually have to challenge and why.
Know when to take appropriate risks with your boss in order to enhancing
your standing with others at the right times and in the right ways.

How much time and energy should you invest in building relationships with
colleagues? Some cultures dictate whether people build their networks
by having lunch together in the cafeteria, regularly meeting for social
events after work, or engaging in informal one-on-one hallway chatter.
The physical setup of a company can influence this (e.g., does your company have enclosed offices or an open-space design?), as can the number of remote locations within a given geography or worldwide. The
approved use of technology (e.g., does your company have high-end video
conferencing or recognize the utility of social networking sites for getting
work done?) can also influence how relationships are managed. Imagine
a totally virtual company where individuals on a team have never met one
another. While it may seem odd to those with many years working in an
office or a cubicle, to the younger generations well versed in social media
and the internet of things, it wouldn't merit a second thought.

Should you be on call when you're on vacation or traveling? Your boss will
have a preference, but your organization's culture may be one in which
people take their vacations and you should not bother them unless it's a
real emergency. Break the established norm when you first arrive in the
role, and you could be seen as an unfeeling taskmaster. In another organization, the expectations are that you need to be on call 24/7. If you don't
respond quickly to a text or email during your vacation, you'll be seen as
a lackadaisical slacker.

When and how should you share recognition and credit with individuals
versus teams? Is recognition a public process (in large groups) or private? Or none at all? How do awards and recognition work and who gets

them? Are only the high potentials recognized for their work? Or are the B players recognized for doing their jobs well because the organization needs to engage them, as they are less likely to get promoted quickly? How are job titles used? Are they given out strategically to recognize people for their contributions or are they strictly tied to specific roles and job levels?

What are the norms regarding social activities during and/or outside of work? Do you need to attend company events and formal dinners when colleagues and superiors invite you? Is joining the informal basketball group on Fridays or playing golf something you simply can't turn down? Should you always be present at town halls, awards presentations, or significant milestone gatherings (e.g., celebrating anniversaries and retirements) or is that only for people who have close relationships to the individuals being honored?

The Intangibles That Influence People's Perception of You

In addition to task indicators and social dynamics, other more intangible elements of an organization's culture can influence your high-potential status. Some may seem rather trivial, but they are quite real. They have to do with the personal intangibles such as appearance (e.g., when you absolutely must wear a jacket or tie or a conservative dress and when you need the right type of jeans to blend in), body language (e.g., when to look intense versus relaxed), style and mannerisms, certain types of phrases to use and/or avoid (we know one company where people cringe at the use of the term "folks" for employees), and, of course, hygiene. Entire books deal with body language alone. And, some people who have all the right capabilities to be senior leaders may derail simply because of a lack of attention to some of these factors (poor hygiene being one of the more egregious).

The criteria seem shallow, of course, and may even border on discriminatory in certain contexts, but they are a reality in the corporate world.

How many CEOs of major corporations look disheveled and sound inarticulate? There is a reason for the massive market for executive coaching, some of which focuses on just "executive grooming" and "presence."

If at some point, you receive feedback about your lack of "executive presence" (a term that often encompasses all of this and more; see chapter 7), take it seriously. It's a sign that your chances of promotion to general management or executive roles are limited. Find out what aspects of "presence" you lack and work on them. Is it your ability to communicate effectively or in compelling ways? Is it your appearance, body language, posture, or something simple enough to change so you more effectively fit in? These elements are important. While they won't get you all the way to the top, they can stop you from getting onto the high-potential list.

Onboarding Yourself into a New Culture

How do you need to adapt behaviorally to cultural factors? For example, do you need to be always adapting or only when you first join an organization? How can you determine what you actually need to adapt to as you onboard? When can you step out on your own and be more of a maverick?

When we talk about the impact of culture on your status as a future high potential, we are generally discussing the process of joining a new company or moving to another operating group within your organization. If you have already been with an organization for several years, you probably have figured out 90 percent of the culture already. That said, norms do vary at different levels in an organization, as they do from one part of the business to another (even function to function or field operating unit to corporate headquarters). The exception is small companies that have consistent norms and values in place, no matter what the level or unit. Attend to the culture at the beginning of each new role beyond your current functional unit or business unit. Once you understand the nuances of the culture, you can simply monitor yourself and your context over time.

If you're new, the formal onboarding process in your organization (or a new part of the business, if you are moving internally) should help you when you join. Unfortunately, organizations are notoriously bad at onboarding in general. Few will actually tell you about the subtleties of their cultural norms. While they may detail the task processes (e.g., this is how we do performance management, this is how our vacation policy works, this is how we do our budgets), it is unlikely that they will provide a list of the cultural dos and don'ts. You must hone your observation skills—watch carefully the norms in behavior in the meetings you attend, how and when people interact with one another—and listen to what office gossip tells you about inappropriate behaviors.

But if you're new and you really want to understand how a culture works, we recommend that you find a culture coach. Some organizations have such coaches who play a formal mentoring role, while others let you fend for yourself. The bottom line is that you need to ensure someone (or a group of people) whom you trust will identify the big behavioral problems to avoid, provide coaching and guidance before you unintentionally step outside the company norms, and help you learn how to earn the right to play at the margins of the culture. Determine immediately who the trustworthy, well-informed individuals are and start to build strong relationships with them. Later on, they are likely to become mentors who will help you in determining your career progression.

Understanding Your Own Approach and Whether You Fit the Culture

How do you navigate the fine line between staying true to yourself versus adapting to the cultural demands in an organization? How far should you go to adapt?

When thinking about how work gets done—all those task indicators we've discussed—start by knowing your own preferences. You want to be highly aware of what you are comfortable adapting to, based partly on your own personality preferences and partly on past experiences. How do you like to do your work and how do you prefer to work with others? Are you someone who likes to work alone and then share your ideas for feedback, or do you prefer iterating and engaging with others as you develop insights and solutions? Do you like working on many different projects at the same time or completing each one in a linear sequence? Do you enjoy cultivating lots of relationships at work or just the handful needed to do your job well? Do you like to socialize with your colleagues outside of work or separate your work and personal relationships? Do you prefer a virtual, remote environment or one where people are always bustling around?

Once you know your own style and preferences, ask yourself the same questions about the organization. Scan the environment and observe how people work together. Are they collaborative, cooperative, or simply coordinated? Do people share ideas and credit with one another, or do they horde information and only parse it out when needed? How do senior leaders recognize others? Are recognition and praise given in public forums or through personal exchanges or both (or not at all)? Do individuals in meetings freely challenge and build upon ideas and recommendations? Or are discussions more orderly, with the formal leader or representatives of the dominant function guiding the discussion? Do people stay connected at all hours of the day and night, or do they shut down after-hours and on vacation? Are tasks done in a very formal step-by-step manner with clear rules and accountabilities or is a creative and organic approach the preferred model for those around you? Do people pre-wire decisions before meetings, or is the real work done in the meetings themselves, with back-door politics frowned upon? Are formalizing roles and accountabilities seen as positive or as a way to undermine you?

Many of these dimensions mirror those we have already discussed. Remember also that corporate culture is like personality; certain aspects are hidden beneath the surface. You only know them after some time and only in certain situations. Just because individuals might tell you how something is supposed to be done, it may not actually be how it gets done. Observing is one of the most reliable means you have to learn your organization's culture. Watch interactions, test your insights with trusted friends and mentors (and culture coaches), and observe with great attention and across many different situations.

Your approach to knowing the social dynamics of the organization should take a similar tactic. First, know yourself. Take a personality test or something similar (many different types of tools are available online for self-development) to help you understand your own disposition for how you like to work. Get greater clarity about your strengths and development needs (hopefully, you have done this already at some point in your career). Then consider how others work together in the organization you are joining. Is the culture based on informal networking or working the hierarchy through more formal protocols? Do people walk the halls and chat about the weekend or does everything happen formally through Outlook calendars? Is there an expectation that only the cool people hang out together after work? Do you need to brush up on your golf or soccer skills to be part of the group? What are the expectations for seeking help, guidance, and feedback from others (e.g., as a leading indicator of openness and a growth mindset, or a sign of weakness)? Determine these quickly in order to maximize your chances of remaining at the top of the talent pipeline. While you may not choose to embrace all (or any) of the cultural norms, know what you are accepting and what you are not. It beats being surprised and derailing without knowing why.

. . .

Culture is complicated. You should pay close attention to it early on and try to detect all the elements we discussed in this chapter. The longer you're with a company, the less you probably have to worry about its culture, since like a fish in water, you've assimilated. That said, an organization's high potentials are often its best exemplars of the cultural traits it values most.

Summary Lessons

- To become and stay a high potential, you need absolute clarity about the cultural demands in both behavior and decision-making style.

- As you climb, you have to not only embody the best of the culture but become a culture carrier.

- For your own happiness and ultimate success, you need to have a strong and positive fit between your own disposition and work preferences and the cultural requirements of your organization.

- As you consider joining a new company and, more importantly, one in a new field or industry, pay attention to the cultural rules. In your job interviews, work hard to identify the cultural norms. Ask yourself how well they fit with you.

- Remember the five cultural areas that have the greatest variability and also have the greatest influence on perceptions of an individual's high-potential capacity: (1) relationships, (2) communications, (3) decision making, (4) individual versus group orientation, and (5) orientation to change. Use these as your frames of reference in your job interviews as well as during your onboarding into a new job.

10

Continuing Your
High-Potential Journey

When GE CEO Jeffrey Immelt commented on the decision to promote John Flannery as the new CEO, he stated very simply, "We didn't put John in place for what he knows. We put him in place *for how fast we think he can learn*" (emphasis ours).[1] We'd like to leave you with this essential insight: *once you stop learning, you stop being a high potential.* At the same time, you have to be acutely aware *of what you need to learn and how best to learn it.*

Your real challenge is not just to become a high potential but also to stay one. The steep curve of the learning challenges you'll encounter only increases as you climb. We've witnessed talented individuals reach the executive level and then lose their status before achieving their ultimate career goal of being a senior vice president or even in the C-suite. Some assumed that the requirement *to earn* their designations no longer applied. After all, they had arrived. Others failed to grasp the new skills and knowledge they needed to develop. Some didn't appreciate that their coping mechanisms for keeping derailers in check were no longer viable. In all these cases, people lost their high-potential designations because they stopped learning in essential ways. We don't want this to happen to you.

We'll start with the bad news—the many ways in which you can lose your high-potential status. Forewarned is forearmed. From there, we turn to a critical question of whether you should leave your organization if you have yet to achieve a high-potential designation. We focus the rest of our discussion on guidance for how best to cultivate the *continuous learning* mindset required to stay a high-potential leader during your entire career.

How Might I Fall Out of My Organization's High-Potential Pool?

People commonly fall out of a high-potential designation. We estimate that between 15 and 25 percent of those with the designation lose their status every year. In the sidebar "How You Can Lose Your High-Potential Status" we have listed the most common reasons we have encountered. Early in your career, a noticeable slide in performance is almost always the primary reason. A lack of composure at key moments or during highly stressful situations can also do you in. As you move upward, behavior and relationships combine with performance to explain the dropouts. The failure to acquire new skills and a greater breadth of perspective play increasingly important roles later on. In our list, you'll recognize a number of our dropout factors as the absence of the five X factors.

Once you achieve high-potential status, you need to work hard to guard your designation. This is where your well-honed situation sensing and career piloting skills will serve you well. In our research, we discovered that it is difficult to reestablish yourself as a high potential after you fall out of the pool. While some organizations may give you a second chance by placing you in another role (called "repotting," as in repotting a plant to see if it grows again), others will simply write you off and focus on other talented individuals. This is especially true at higher levels. Once you are perceived as a "solid performer" or as a difficult or needy or a self-serving person, you will find it hard to shake off those perceptions, even if you succeed in miraculously turning around your performance or behavior. In our interviews, we heard about the occasional case of

HOW YOU CAN LOSE YOUR HIGH-POTENTIAL STATUS

- You consistently underperform in the various responsibilities of your role or you fail to deliver on one or more critical performance goals that were expected of you. If you miss key objectives more than once, you will no longer be a high potential.

- You deliver on all your objectives, but your results don't have the broad impact on the organization that they should have had (or that your boss and other senior executives expected you to have).

- You receive consistent feedback from your direct reports and/or peers that they don't enjoy working with you. They make it known to superiors that you are a poor, difficult, absent, or arrogant manager or colleague. The opposite outcome of the talent accelerating X factor.

- You create the impression that you are too driven, ambitious, aggressive, and self-serving in your career aspirations. Someone who does this is labeled as "chasing the level"—seeking promotions rather than furthering the business.

- You consistently clash with your boss about work styles or you simply neglect to effectively manage upward, failing to demonstrate the situation sensing X factor in action.

- You lack executive presence, however that is defined in your organization (e.g., disorganized, underdressed for meetings, poor attention to body language, lack of ability to speak clearly and with authority).

- You fail to present and communicate your ideas well in meetings, our X factor of complexity translating.

- Your colleagues perceive that your insights and ideas lack relevance. In short, others think you are not connecting the dots in ways that matter.

- You constantly arrive late to meetings, miss deadlines, or otherwise prove to be unreliable. People need to be able to count on you to deliver, especially your boss.

- You lose emotional control, often get openly frustrated, and show your negative emotions too frequently. People know when you are upset and how to push your buttons.

- You forget to pay attention to the politics and culture of the organization and the way people are expected to communicate upward to senior leaders (situation sensing).

- You fail to treat others with respect and listen well. We commonly see this, particularly among with people strong egos and/or low emotional intelligence.

- You show poor judgment when given sensitive or confidential information (e.g., by sharing it with the wrong people at the wrong times). Remember the old adage, "three people can keep a secret if two of them are dead."

- You fail to learn the skills and knowledge that are imperatives demanded by the roles into which you could be promoted—our X factor of catalytic learning.

someone returning to high-potential status after a major misstep, but it always required the individual to demonstrate truly exceptional performance and/or a highly visible behavioral change. In addition, the person needed a few keen advocates among influential superiors who were willing to go to bat and argue for their dramatically improved performance.

If you've fallen from grace, you will find it very hard to regain your high-potential status. This doesn't mean that the organization doesn't value you; it just no longer sees you rising to senior levels. If this happens, what should you do? We recommend you do the same things as any other solid performer who hasn't been labeled a high performer: talk to your boss, your boss's boss, HR, and other leaders. In the next section, we advise about what to listen for, what to ask for, and then how to decide when is the right time to move on.

What Should I Do If I Haven't Yet Received a High-Potential Designation?

What if you've not been designated a high potential, even though you've been working on all the X factors? Don't worry just yet. Remember, as we discussed in chapter 1, many companies have a formal policy not to tell employees their status. There are signs, however, such as extra attention from senior leaders or being asked to join special task forces or attend leadership programs, that indicate you may be on the high-potential list. But what if you aren't seeing any of those signs? While many elements come into play in how an organization determines potential, there are ways you can get a glimpse into your long-term prospects.

What to Listen For in Conversations with Higher-Ups

Aside from outright performance issues or style clashes, you can get a sense about your trajectory in your conversations with others and through keen observation about how your boss is treating your peers (and how you are expected to treat your own people who may have designations as high potentials themselves). Talk to your boss, your boss's boss, your mentors, and your HR person, in particular, about your career goals and aspirations. While you should never overplay your ambition, others should know what you are thinking and where you want to go in the future (and it's important input into the talent management process, as discussed in chapter 8). If your chance of becoming a high potential is minimal (and many organizations are not transparent about this), these people will use three different tactics to convey messages that generally indicate you are not heading toward a high-potential future in your company, at least for the foreseeable future. These tactics are *indifference, placation,* and *misdirection.*

The first—indifference—is perhaps the easiest to spot when discussing your career aspirations with others. Simply put, they will politely listen to your interests but will not convey a sense of excitement or enthusiasm about them. In the best-case scenario, you will receive a calm, measured response thanking you for conveying the information and duly noting it. In the worst case, they will probably just stare at you dispassionately and promptly change the subject. When that happens, you obviously know you're not going very far in this organization.

The tactic of placation is much more commonly used, particularly with high-performing B players. In this case, your bosses are interested in keeping you with the company—after all, you are doing great work—but they don't see much potential to grow into bigger roles at higher levels in the company. They would rather you take on other lateral roles or stay in your current job and continue to perform well (often the case with people who have deep expertise). As a result, they will likely tell you that you are highly valued and doing great in your current role. They may tell you that you need to continue to demonstrate your contribution and/or that "these things take time." You may also hear that there is always room in the company for people like you, with your skill set, and at your level. Perhaps they will even say that there will be other opportunities for you in the future, though they are unlikely to promise anything at higher levels.

The tactic of misdirection, on the other hand, is more difficult to spot and can be easily confused with real positive message about being a high potential. In these cases, your bosses might tell you about new experiences you can gain, new developmental areas you can work on after you've shown improvements in those previously identified, or potential future roles they have in mind for you, even alternative potential career paths they can see you in downstream. In short, you think you might be a high potential from the message, but the story keeps changing. They want you to stay, continue to develop, and add value to the company, just not in more senior positions. Given our discussion about herky-jerky career paths and the need to learn from different experiences (chapters 4 and 6), however, you can see how these messages could be very similar to or even the same as those given to legitimate high-potential talent.

Your goal is to honestly convey your long-term career goals and read between the lines to determine how your bosses really see you. You might even ask the question, "What do you see as my long-term career destination at this time?" If the company sees that you have significant potential, you are likely to be showered with a wealth of positive messages about your level of stretch and future opportunities with phrases like "We have big plans for you" "We think you can go places and do lots of things" or "We'll all be working for you one day." If, on the other hand, you are not in the running, they'll use one of the three tactics we've described. The organization is not trying to dupe you. It is interested in continuing to invest in you, just not in the same exact way as those who it feels have more potential.

What to Ask For

What happens if you do determine that your potential is limited? Whether your bosses tell you directly or not, ask what you need to do concretely to be more successful. What do you need to demonstrate to be seen as having the potential or ability to take on larger roles or greater responsibility? Get them to be as specific as possible. If their comments are not about current performance, odds are that one or more of the X factors will be part of the equation.

For example, you could have an issue of fit with your boss or your boss's boss, which is influencing their point of view (situation sensing). Maybe there are negative rumors about how you interact with others or the quality of the talent you have brought in or managed (talent accelerating). You may have not demonstrated what you needed to in a challenging assignment in the way they expected (career piloting), or perhaps your communication and strategic skills are not yet strong enough to influence senior leaders (complexity translating). Or you might not be demonstrating the ability to learn and grow from experiences or an inherent interest in building your own capabilities (catalytic learning).

Even if you have demonstrated all of these X factors, there is still the nuance of cultural fit to consider. Perhaps you simply don't match the dominant style of your organization and have as yet been unable or unwilling to change your behavior enough to fit in. These are the insights you need to gather from the discussions and your own observations. By doing so, you can determine where to focus your efforts to be seen as a high potential now and in the future, whether with your current organization or elsewhere.

Should I Consider Leaving My Organization?

Although you've been told or you sense that you are not a high potential and your future progression is limited, knowing this information does give you some choices. Specifically, you can decide to keep performing at your best with the hopes that the situation will change for the better (e.g., you get a new boss, a new role and sponsors in a different function or part of the business, a favorable assessment, or your skills simply improve), or you can leave and look elsewhere. While exiting and starting fresh somewhere else might seem the easiest option at times, ask yourself the following questions first.

How many bosses have you had to date? If just one, it is likely premature to jump to another organization. If three or four, and none have been advocates who designated you as a high potential, this is a serious sign that you should look elsewhere. This is particularly true if you always are slotted in the "solid performer" box in your annual reviews. At the same time, you have to ask yourself whether you feel your performance has been more exceptional than their perceptions indicate: "How does my work ethic stack up to my peers?", "How does my personal talent compare?", "How do my work outcomes compare—and do I have tangible and visible comparisons to make a case?"

Be sure you are familiar with how the talent review and promotions processes work. Is your data current? Do people really know your career aspirations? What is the emphasis in your firm on tenure versus other factors? How important is formal education for higher roles (e.g., graduate degrees and executive education)? Have you been formally assessed in your leadership behaviors or is there a way in which you can request feedback on your skills and capabilities? Are there development programs you can participate in for further growth to demonstrate your commitment and interest in the company?

Finally, take a hard look at your own motivation. Have you been giving it your all? Have you been consistently mastering and demonstrating the X factors? These are all important considerations before simply leaving because you are unclear about what the company thinks about your potential. We have known many cases, for example, where someone resigned, only to learn when they handed in their resignation paperwork or informed their boss of their intent that they were, in fact, a high potential. A new, exciting development experience or promotion was just about to be offered to them.

Let's say that after considering all these variables, you decide to look at outside opportunities, and you start receiving offers. There are several critical factors to weigh as you consider your options. Is the next organization's culture a highly positive fit for you? Go back to our discussion (chapter 9) of culture to assess which dimensions feel like the more natural fit, for example, relational versus individualistic. Do the organization's career processes look more progressive or better suited to what you want than your current one? Is the job itself a strong fit, playing well to your innate talents, capabilities, and experience to date? What can you take with you to the new firm in terms of experiences, skills, and relationships? Will any of these provide you with an initial performance advantage? What will you learn from the new role and organization that could be valuable to your career? What will you end up leaving behind at your last organization in terms of networks of relationships, mentors, high-quality teammates, and training or mentoring opportunities? Will giving these up put you at a performance disadvantage in starting out in your new role?

Leaving your industry can often mean starting over when it comes to your network of relationships as well as a steep learning curve in knowledge demands. We do know from research on career portability that only certain factors are portable to jobs on the outside. These can include your personal relationships with clients and outside networks, your training and education, and your innate talents. So it is important to critically assess how much of an advantage these will be in your new organization.

Staying a High Potential by Focusing on Feedback and Development

You've been designated a high potential, and you continue to practice the five X factors and do all the things we've recommended. Now what? As we said at the beginning of this chapter, your challenge is to keep learning and growing. This is the essence of our fifth X factor, catalytic learning, and why we say that catalytic learning undergirds all of the other X factors. You simply must keep learning.

Learn through Feedback

Over the last two decades, we have learned a great deal about leadership development as it relates to high-potential talent. At the core is the importance of self-awareness and feedback. Leaders who are self-aware are simply better performers and in turn have higher potential. This quality is a cornerstone of what we call emotional intelligence. In one study comparing star performing senior leaders with average ones, Daniel Goleman concluded that nearly 90 percent of the difference could be attributed to emotional intelligence versus cognitive abilities.[2]

Feedback serves as both a way to understand and diagnose your strengths and opportunities for improvement, and a powerful means for driving change. It is essential to self-awareness. If you learn from a feedback report that your peers find you difficult to work with, your direct reports don't see you as inspirational, and your boss rates you poorly on judgment, then you clearly have areas to focus on for the future before you achieve the next level. Conversely, when you learn that you are strong at building teams, leading large transformational efforts, and selecting great talent, those indicate a great future senior leader. The question then becomes, "Should I focus my energies on my shortcomings or my strengths?"

The simple answer is it's not an either-or, but both. Research by John Zenger, Joseph Folkman, Robert Sherwin, and Barbara Steel indicates that a focus on building your strengths generally has a greater return in terms of performance impact than working on shortcomings, with some key exceptions.[3] Based on a sample of the 360-degree feedback surveys of over 20,000 managers and over 200,000 respondents, their data shows that only 28 percent of these individuals had critical weaknesses that had to be addressed developmentally. They offered two self-assessment questions to help you decide whether to address a weakness:

- Have I received feedback in any credible form that suggests a habit or harmful behavior is holding me back in my performance or career?

- Am I aware of any negative perceptions of my behavior that might be overshadowing my good qualities? Are any of these behaviors often top of mind for those I work with and do they constitute what colleagues would say is part of my personal brand?

If the answer to either of these is yes, then you need to make it your highest priority to tackle that weakness or harmful behavior without delay. Managers in the sample who possessed one or more fatal shortcomings were rated at the seventeenth percentile in terms of effectiveness. This is why a focus on derailers can be critically important, particularly at more senior levels in the organization. An overused strength can also become an opportunity for improvement or even a derailer later in your career.

Our guidance, after providing feedback and assessment results to thousands of leaders at all levels and stages of their careers, is that it's most effective to help them identify strengths to build on *and* opportunities to improve. The weighting depends more on your role and the content on which you are being measured. For example, if you are low in any of our X factors, you should focus on improving in those areas as well as capitalizing on those where you are already doing well.

In the end, if you want to become and remain a high potential through-out your career, it is paramount that you actively seek ongoing feedback not only on what to develop but on your progress against your goals. When Marshall Goldsmith and Howard Morgan investigated the activities that had the greatest impact on leadership development, this was the one that consistently emerged time and time again as the most valuable.[4] Those leaders who discussed their development priorities with their colleagues and then consistently achieved them showed the most striking improvements over time. In contrast, managers who did not discuss their improvement needs and goals with colleagues showed improvement that hardly exceeded random chance.

How to Solicit Feedback

Some final questions that are the bases for continuous learning and our most fundamental premise to being a high potential now and in the future are: How are you seeking candid feedback? And from whom? How are you prioritizing your development efforts and tracking your progress? Do you even know what you need to work on and enhance for the future? Are you in constant-learning mode and do you connect the dots? Do you have a passion for learning and improving your own capabilities and knowledge as a leader?

Following are a few formal and informal ways in which you can solicit feedback to help you pinpoint your strengths and development opportunities, as well as track your progress.

Always start with your boss. Research has shown that your boss is often in the best position to know what areas will require your focus and attention. Your boss determines both your performance ratings and your status as a high potential. This is the crux of our situation sensing X factor. Without good rapport with and reading of your manager, you simply won't get the feedback you need.

Ask direct reports and/or peers for feedback. Following a team meeting, conference call, or project debriefing, ask outright for constructive feedback. The information you receive, however, may be biased because they are telling you directly to your face. Some people don't like to give feedback or address issues this way, and your direct reports may feel threatened by telling you where you need to improve as a leader and manager. A better way to gather colleagues' feedback is through confidential tools, such as an online 360-degree feedback survey (see chapter 7). Use your company's formal HR tools (if available) or via an outside coach or provider. By collecting data independently and sharing the results with you in an aggregate manner (to protect confidentiality of respondents), colleagues are likely to be much more candid and open in telling you what you really need to work on to improve. This process might be more painful to you as a recipient of the feedback, but it will also be far more accurate and helpful.

Partner with a mentor, coach, or another colleague. Someone you work with regularly or perhaps an external expert you hire to shadow you for a day can work with you and give you real-time feedback. Or you might develop a long-term coaching relationship with someone who can give you developmental insights. Even an internal mentor who can report any buzz about you can help in choosing those developmental areas that you should further address and where you need to close major gaps. When selecting someone to help you, pick a person you trust and who has your best interests at heart. In the end, focus on developing yourself as a future leader. If you look carefully, you will find that many, including your organization, share your goals.

. . .

This book is about taking charge of your career. We hope that the information helps you achieve your goals and that you make progress on the path to reaching your full potential as a leader. Good luck on your journey!

Notes

Chapter 1

1. A. H. Church and J. Waclawski, "Take the Pepsi Challenge: Talent Development at PepsiCo," in *Strategy-Driven Talent Management: A Leadership Imperative*, ed. R. Silzer and B. E. Dowell, SIOP Professional Practice Series (San Francisco: Jossey-Bass, 2010), 617–640.

2. J. A. Conger and G. Pillans, *Rethinking Talent Management* (London: The Corporate Research Forum, 2016).

3. A. H. Church, C. T. Rotolo, N. M. Ginther, and R. Levine, "How Are Top Companies Designing and Managing Their High-Potential Programs? A Follow-up Talent Management Benchmark Study," *Consulting Psychology Journal: Practice and Research* 67, no. 1 (2015): 17–47.

4. R. Silzer and A. H. Church, "The Pearls and Perils of Identifying Potential," *Industrial and Organizational Psychology: Perspectives on Science and Practice* 2 (2009): 377–412.

5. A. H. Church and R. Silzer, "Going Behind the Corporate Curtain with a Blueprint for Leadership Potential: An Integrated Framework for Identifying High-Potential Talent," *People & Strategy* 36, no. 4 (2014): 51–58.

6. A. H. Church and C. T. Rotolo, "How Are Top Companies Assessing Their High-Potentials and Senior Executives? A Talent Management Benchmark Study," *Consulting Psychology Journal: Practice and Research* 65, no. 3 (2013): 199–223; Church et al., "How Are Top Companies Designing and Managing Their High-Potential Programs?"; R. Silzer and H. Church, "Identifying and Assessing High Potential Talent: Current Organizational Practices," in *Strategy-Driven Talent Management*, 213–279; and D. A. Ready, J. A. Conger, and L. A. Hill, "Are You a High Potential?" *Harvard Business Review*, June 2010.

Chapter 2

1. D. A. Ready, J. A. Conger, and L. A. Hill, "Are You a High Potential?" *Harvard Business Review*, June 2010.

2. Ibid.

Chapter 3

1. E. Michaels, H. Handfield-Jones, and B. Axelrod, *The War for Talent* (Boston: Harvard Business School Press, 2001).

2. R. Goffee and G. R. Jones, *Why Should Anyone Be Led by You? What It Takes to Be an Authentic Leader* (Boston: Harvard Business School Press, 2006).

Chapter 4

1. "Seeking Their Fortune: The Career Path for Top Executives in Big Companies," *Knowledge@Wharton*, February 11, 2014, http://knowledge.wharton.upenn.edu/article/seeking-fortune-career-path-top-executives-big-companies. See also P. Cappelli, M. Hamori, and R. Bonet, "Who's Got Those Top Jobs?" *Harvard Business Review*, March 2014.

2. "Seeking Their Fortune: The Career Path for Top Executives in Big Companies."

3. J. J. Gabarro, "When a New Manager Takes Charge," *Harvard Business Review*, January 2007.

4. R. S. Kaplan, "What to Ask the Person in the Mirror," *Harvard Business Review*, January 2007.

5. Gabarro, "When a New Manager Takes Charge."

6. M. D. Watkins, *The First 90 Days: Proven Strategies for Getting Up to Speed Faster and Smarter* (rev. ed.) (Boston: Harvard Business Review Press, 2013).

7. Gabarro, "When a New Manager Takes Charge."

8. Watkins, *The First 90 Days*.

Chapter 5

1. G. Shaw, R. Brown, and P. Bromiley, "Strategic Stories: How 3M Is Rewriting Business Planning," *Harvard Business Review*, May 1998.

Chapter 6

1. M. W. McCall Jr., *High Flyers: Developing the Next Generation of Leaders* (Boston: Harvard Business School Press, 1998).

2. M. M. Lombardo and R. W. Eichinger, "High Potentials as High Learners," *Human Resource Management* 39, no. 4 (Winter 2000): 3.

3. C. Dweck, *Mindset: The New Psychology of Success* (New York: Ballantine Books, 2008).

4. Ibid., 10.

5. Jim Collins, *Good to Great: Why Some Companies Make the Leap . . . and Others Don't* (New York: HarperCollins, 2001).

6. Dweck, *Mindset*, 111–112.

7. M. Seligman, *Learned Optimism: How to Change Your Mind and Life* (New York, Pocket Books, 1990).

8. S. G. Barsade, "The Ripple Effect: Emotional Contagion and Its Influence on Group Behavior," *Administrative Science Quarterly* 47, no. 4 (December 2002): 644–675.

9. R. Cross and R. Thomas, "A Smarter Way to Network," *Harvard Business Review*, July–August 2011.

10. K. A. Ericsson, M. J. Prietula, and E. T. Cokely, "The Making of an Expert," *Harvard Business Review*, July–August 2007.

11. Ibid.

12. Jascha Heifetz website, jaschaheifetz.com/about/quotations, accessed August 7, 2017.

13. Juan Ramón Alaix, "The CEO of Zoetis on How He Prepared for the Top Job," *Harvard Business Review*, June 2014.

14. Ibid, 4.

15. Ibid, 5.

Chapter 7

1. A. H. Church and C. T. Rotolo, "How Are Top Companies Assessing Their High-Potentials and Senior Executives? A Talent Management Benchmark Study," *Consulting Psychology Journal: Practice and Research* 65, no. 3 (2013): 199–223.

2. A. H. Church and C. T. Rotolo, "Lifting the Veil: What Happens When You Are Transparent with People about Their Future Potential?" *People + Strategy* 39, no. 4 (2016): 36–40.

3. Ibid.

4. Church and Rotolo, "How Are Top Companies Assessing Their High-Potentials and Senior Executives?"

5. A. H. Church, "Managerial Self-Awareness in High-Performing Individuals in Organizations," *Journal of Applied Psychology* 82, no. 2 (1997): 281–292.

6. A. H. Church, C. T. Rotolo, N. M. Ginther, and R. Levine, "How Are Top Companies Designing and Managing Their High-Potential Programs? A Follow-Up Talent Management Benchmark Study," *Consulting Psychology Journal: Practice and Research* 67, no. 1 (2015): 17–47.

Chapter 10

1. E. Crooks, "GE's Immelt: 'Every Job Looks Easy When You're Not the One Doing It,'" *Financial Times*, June 12, 2017.

2. D. Goleman, "What Makes a Leader?" *Harvard Business Review*, January 2004.

3. J. H. Zenger, J. R. Folkman, R. H. Sherwin, Jr., and B. A. Steel, *How to Be Exceptional: Drive Leadership Success by Magnifying Your Strengths* (New York: McGraw-Hill Education, 2012).

4. M. Goldsmith and H. Morgan, "Leadership Is a Contact Sport: The 'Follow-up Factor' in Management Development," *Strategy + Business* 36, August 25, 2004.

Bibliography

References

Church, A. H. "Managerial Self-Awareness in High-Performing Individuals in Organizations." *Journal of Applied Psychology* 82 (1997): 281–292.

Church, A. H., and C. T. Rotolo. "How Are Top Companies Assessing Their High-Potentials and Senior Executives? A Talent Management Benchmark Study." *Consulting Psychology Journal: Practice and Research* 65, no. 3 (2013): 199–223.

Church, A. H., and C. T. Rotolo. "Lifting the Veil: What Happens When You Are Transparent with People about Their Future Potential?" *People & Strategy* 39, no. 4 (2016): 36–40.

Church, A. H., C. T. Rotolo, N. M. Ginther, and R. Levine. "How Are Top Companies Designing and Managing Their High-Potential Programs? A Follow-up Talent Management Benchmark Study." *Consulting Psychology Journal: Practice and Research* 67, no. 1 (2015): 17–47.

Church, A. H., and R. Silzer. "Going Behind the Corporate Curtain with a Blueprint for Leadership Potential: An Integrated Framework for Identifying High-Potential Talent." *People & Strategy* 36 (2014): 51–58.

Dweck, C. S. *Mindset: The New Psychology of Success.* New York: Random House, 2006.

Ready, D. A., J. A. Conger, and L. A. Hill. "Are You a High Potential?" *Harvard Business Review,* June 2010, 78–84.

Silzer, R., and A. H. Church. "The Pearls and Perils of Identifying Potential." *Industrial and Organizational Psychology: Perspectives on Science and Practice* 2 (2009): 377–412.

Additional Helpful References

Bracken, D. W., and A. H. Church. "The 'New' Performance Management Paradigm: Capitalizing on the Unrealized Potential of 360 Degree Feedback." *People & Strategy* 36, no. 2 (2013): 34–40.

Burke, W. W., and D. A. Noumair. "The Role of Personality Assessment in Organization Development." In *Organization Development: A Data-Driven Approach to Organizational Change,* edited by J. Waclawski and A. H. Church, 55–77. San Francisco: Jossey-Bass, 2002.

Carey, D. C. and D. Ogden. "CEO Succession Planning: Ensuring Leadership at the Top." In *The Talent Management Handbook: Creating Organizational Excellence by Identifying, Developing, and Promoting Your Best People,* edited by L. A. Berger and D. R. Berger, 243–252. New York: McGraw-Hill, 2004.

Charan, R., D. Carey, and M. Useem. *Boards That Lead: When to Take Charge, When to Partner, and When to Stay Out of the Way*. Boston: Harvard Business Review Press, 2014.

Church, A. H. "A New Understanding of Potential: Do You Really Know Who the High-Potentials Are in Your Organization?" *Talent Quarterly* 1 (2014): 15–19.

Church, A. H. "The Pursuit of Potential: Six Things You Need to Know about Defining Potential in Your Organization." *Talent Quarterly* 6 (2015): 29–35.

Church, A. H. "What Do We Know about Developing Leadership Potential? The Role of OD in Strategic Talent Management." *OD Practitioner* 46, no. 3 (2014): 52–61.

Church, A. H., and S. Dutta. "The Promise of Big Data for OD: Old Wine in New Bottles or the Next Generation of Data-Driven Methods for Change?" *OD Practitioner* 45, no. 4 (2013): 23–31.

Church, A. H., C. R. Fleck, G. C. Foster, R. C. Levine, F. J. Lopez, and C. T. Rotolo. "Does Purpose Matter? The Stability of Personality Assessments in Organization Development and Talent Management Applications over Time." *Journal of Applied Behavioral Science* 52, no. 4 (2016): 1–32.

Church, A. H., and C. T. Rotolo. "The Role of the Individual in Self-Assessment for Leadership Development." In *Self-Management and Leadership Development*, edited by M. G. Rothstein and R. J. Burke, 25–61. Cheltenham, Glasgow, UK: Edward Elgar Publishing Limited, 2010.

Church, A. H., and R. Silzer. "Are We on the Same Wavelength? Four Steps for Moving from Talent Signals to Valid Talent Management Applications." *Industrial and Organizational Psychology: Perspectives on Science and Practice* 9, no. 3 (2016): 645–654.

Church, A. H., and J. Waclawski. "The Relationship between Individual Personality Orientation and Executive Leadership Behavior." *Journal of Occupational & Organizational Psychology* 71 (1998): 99–125.

Church, A. H., and J. Waclawski. "Take the Pepsi Challenge: Talent Development at PepsiCo." In *Strategy-Driven Talent Management: A Leadership Imperative*, edited by R. Silzer and B. E. Dowell, 617–640. San Francisco, Jossey-Bass, 2010.

Church, A. H., J. Waclawski, and W. W. Burke. "Multisource Feedback for Organization Development and Change." In *The Handbook of Multisource Feedback: The Comprehensive Resource for Designing and Implementing MSF Processes*, edited by D. W. Bracken, C. W. Timmreck, and A. H. Church, 301–317. San Francisco: Jossey-Bass, 2001.

Conaty, B., and R. Charan. *The Talent Masters: Why Smart Leaders Put People before Numbers*. New York: Crown Business, 2010.

Highhouse, S. "Assessing the Candidate as a Whole: A Historical and Critical Analysis of Individual Psychological Assessment for Personnel Decision Making." *Personnel Psychology* 55 (2002): 363–396.

McCauley, C. D., and M. W. McCall Jr., eds. *Using Experience to Develop Leadership Talent: How Organizations Leverage On-the-Job Development*. San Francisco: Jossey-Bass, 2014.

Meister, J. C., and K. Willyerd. *The 2020 Workplace: How Innovative Companies Attract, Develop, and Keep Tomorrow's Employees Today*. New York: HarperCollins, 2010.

Michaels, E., H. Handfield-Jones, and B. Axelrod. *The War for Talent*. Boston: Harvard Business School Press, 2001.

Nowack, K. M., and S. Mashihi. "Evidence-Based Answers to 15 Questions about Leveraging 360-Degree Feedback." *Consulting Psychology Journal: Practice and Research* 64, no. 5 (2012): 157–182.

Ruddy, T., and J. Anand. "Managing Talent in Global Organizations." In *Strategy-Driven Talent Management: A Leadership Imperative*, edited by R. Silzer and B. E. Dowell, 549–593. San Francisco: Jossey-Bass, 2010.

Scott, J. C., and D. H. Reynolds, eds. *The Handbook of Workplace Assessment: Evidence Based Practices for Selecting and Developing Organizational Talent.* San Francisco: Jossey-Bass, 2010.

Silzer, R., and H. Church. "Identifying and Assessing High Potential Talent: Current Organizational Practices." In *Strategy-Driven Talent Management: A Leadership Imperative,* edited by R. Silzer and B. E. Dowell, 213–279, SIOP Professional Practice Series. San Francisco: Jossey-Bass, 2010.

Silzer, R., and B. E. Dowell, eds. *Strategy-Driven Talent Management: A Leadership Imperative.* San Francisco: Jossey-Bass, 2010.

Sperry, L. "Executive Coaching and Leadership Assessment: Past, Present, and Future." *Consulting Psychology Journal: Practice and Research* 65, no. 4 (2013): 284–288.

Stamoulis, D. *Senior Executive Assessment: A Key to Responsible Corporate Governance.* Chichester, West Sussex, United Kingdom: John Wiley & Sons, Ltd., 2009.

Thornton III, G. C., G. P. Hollenbeck, and S. K. Johnson. "Selecting Leaders: Executives and High-Potentials." In *Handbook of Employee Selection,* edited by J. L. Farr and N. T. Tippins, 823–840. New York: Routledge, Taylor, & Francis Group, 2010.

Van Velsor, E., S. Taylor, and J. B. Leslie. "An Examination of the Relationships among Self-Perception Accuracy, Self-Awareness, Gender, and Leader Effectiveness." *Human Resource Management* 32, nos. 2–3 (1993): 249–263.

Index

Acknowledgments

The idea for this book began with a call from our agent, Jill Marsal. She had read our HBR article, "Are You a High Potential?" and asked if we had considered writing a book on the topic. We hadn't. Her call, however, inspired us to start writing. So first and foremost, we'd like to thank Jill for her foresight and encouragement. Jay would also like to thank his colleagues Doug Ready and Linda Hill for the research and writing partnership that produced the HBR article, which in turn laid the groundwork for this book. Jay is especially grateful to Doug for their many years of researching and writing together to address pressing talent issues facing organizations. It has been a rewarding partnership and friendship.

We feel so fortunate to have had our gifted editor at Harvard Business Review Press, Melinda Merino, as an influential partner on this project. It would be an understatement to say how lucky we are. Melinda brings out the best in us as authors, whether that's brainstorming the book's structure, honing our narrative voice, or ensuring a clear sense of focus in each chapter. Her sense of humor and willingness to listen made the journey enjoyable and productive. Melinda's colleagues at the Press, Jane Gebhart and Dave Lievens, have been instrumental in making our words flow beautifully, untangling complex points, and keeping us on track. Thank you both. We also want to recognize Keith Pfeffer and his colleagues on the Press's sales and marketing team. We are excited to work with you as our book becomes a reality.

This is the first time the two of us have partnered on a writing project. We proved to be great complements to one another on the many demands of writing a book like this one. Allan extends a special thanks to Jay for inviting him to join this project and for the creative energy we shared. Jay is especially grateful to Allan for his critical thinking, his impressive depth of expertise in high-potential assessments, and his good-hearted willingness to put up with Jay's constant editing. It's been a fantastic journey!

This book would not have been possible without the many individuals who so generously shared their insights and experiences about high-potential talent and leadership with us. Allan would like to thank his current and former bosses at PepsiCo, including Lucien Alziari, Peggy Moore, David Ayre, Ron Parker, Andrea Ferrara, David Henderson, Sergio Ezama, Monique Ritacca-Herena, Ruth Fattori, and Cynthia Trudell. Each of these people challenged him and contributed something unique to his knowledge of the inner workings of talent development and human potential in organizations. He would also like to thank his close colleagues, Chris Rotolo, Rebecca Levine, Nicole Ginther, Mike Tuller, Matt Del Giudice, Alyson Margulies, Cara Wade, Kim Happich, Christina Fleck, Lily Maissen, Lori Dawson, Jamie Lopez, Rafi Prager, Linn Nordlander, Jacqueline Dickey, David Oliver, Jeff Johnson, Miguel Premoli, Camilla Arnsten, Christopher Shyrock, and Pavan Bhatia, with whom he worked to build a world-class assessment and development system.

In addition, Allan wants to recognize his external co-conspirators, friends, influencers, and at times intellectual sparring partners on the subject of talent management and everything high potential, including John Scott, Karen Paul, Dave Bracken, John Boudreau, Rodney Warrenfeltz, Jeff McHenry, Bill Macey, Steven Rogelberg, Alan Colquitt, Morgan McCall, Cindy McCauley, Allen Kraut, Milt Hakel, Allen Kamen, Wayne Cascio, Charlie and Evelyn Rogers, Paul Russell, Carol Surface, Maurice Cox, Joel Brockner, Doug Reynolds, Elaine Pulakos, Debra Noumair, Bernardo Ferdman, Eric Elder, Carol Timmreck, Peter Cairo, David Dotlich, Steve Krupp, Marc Effron, Tomas Chamorro-Premuzic, and Seymour Adler. A special thanks to Rob Silzer for all the discussion, theoretical debates, and partnership regarding the underlying nature of leadership potential and the foundational work behind the Leadership Potential BluePrint. Rob made Allan see the potential in "potential."

Jay would like to thank Joyce Rowland for the opportunity to work with her and her organization on talent development opportunities over many years. These opportunities, combined with Joyce's keen insights about talent, have been instrumental in a number of the lessons contained in this book. Jay also wishes to express his gratitude to his colleagues in the HR and leadership development communities who contributed important insights: Mark Alders, Scott Dolny, Steve Erickson, Brian Fishel, Helena Gottschling, Allan Kaye, Lacey Leone, Grace MacArthur, Amy Meyer, Nagrath Moheet, Michael Molinaro, Janette Piankoff, David Rodriquez, Richard Vosburgh, Rebecca Walker, Kevin Wilde, and Ian Ziskin.

A number of executives and CEOs played particularly important roles in deepening our wisdom related to the X factors and high-potential leaders. A special thank-you goes to Ray Bennet, Scott Drury, Werner Geissler, Melanie Healey, Steve Klar, Jeff Martin, Robbie Pearl, Douglas Peterson, Dimitri Panayotopoulos, Drew Pinto, Debra Reed, Brendon Swords, Steven Williams, and Martha Wyrsch. In addition, extensive interviews with the following individuals deepened our understanding of what it takes to become and stay a high potential: Joel Albarella, Brenda Arends, Hari Avula, Arnoud Balhuizen, Jeremy Chura, Claudia Craigoza, Jim Cristallo, Elan Feldman, Gina Fu, Kelly Hall, Graeme Hepworth, Jean Hyman, John Jenkins, Chris Kempczinski, Veena Khanna, Spencer Li, Julian Lustig, Jim Lynch, Janisse Martinez, Rachel Sommers, Divya Vishwanath, Matt Thompson, Matthew Milcetich, Amy Miller, Rob Speranza, Don Swan, Greg Veith, and Grace Warren. In addition, there have been many other women and men who, over the years, have shared their leadership experiences with us. While only a few of them are featured in the book, we deeply appreciate the lessons they have taught us.

Both of us wish to acknowledge and thank the mentors who influenced our insights in this book and ultimately our careers. Jack Gabarro, John Kotter, and Paul Lawrence played important roles in Jay's understanding of the complexity of leadership and the critical value of field-based research. More importantly, they taught him that research needs to advance management practice in significant ways. Ralph Biggadike, John Kotter, and Jack Weber inspired Jay to become a professor of organization behavior, to discover his love for teaching managers, and to pursue his passion around leadership. Jay's research with Ed Lawler was the catalyst for his interest in the human resources function and talent management. Warner Burke took Allan under his wing when he first entered the field of organization development and has continued his mentorship throughout Allan's career. We are grateful to these special individuals who have shaped our thinking and our careers. In closing, Jay would also like to thank Claremont McKenna College for the sabbatical that provided him the gift of time to write this book.

About the Authors

JAY A. CONGER is the Henry R. Kravis Chaired Professor of Leadership Studies at Claremont McKenna College. As an executive educator and management coach, he has worked with thousands of leaders over his career. His passion for teaching has led to rankings as one of the world's top management educators by prominent business publications. Drawing upon his consulting and research on leadership, Jay has published fifteen books and over one hundred articles on topics ranging from the development of leaders, persuasion and communications, executive leadership, boardroom governance, and organizational change. He is a frequent contributor to *Harvard Business Review,* and his HBR article, "The Necessary Art of Persuasion," is a longtime bestseller. His insights on leadership have been featured in *Businessweek,* the *Economist,* the *Financial Times, Forbes, Fortune,* the *New York Times,* the *San Francisco Chronicle,* and the *Wall Street Journal.*

Over his career Jay has served on the management faculties of the Harvard Business School, INSEAD (France), the London Business School, McGill University, and the University of Southern California. He is the former faculty chair of the Kravis Leadership Institute at Claremont McKenna College, where he led one of the nation's leading academic centers for leadership development and research. He was also the faculty director of the Leadership Institute at the University of Southern California's Marshall School of Business.

His passion for leadership began at a young age. Early on, Jay sought out opportunities to lead, first as a student, and later as an organizer for political campaigns, an international marketing manager, a professor, and a consultant. He received a BA from Dartmouth College, an MBA from the University of Virginia, and his doctorate from Harvard Business School.

ALLAN H. CHURCH is Senior Vice President of Global Talent Assessment & Development at PepsiCo. He is responsible for setting the enterprise talent strategy for high-potential identification and development, as well as for strengthening the leadership pipeline via the People Planning talent review process. Allan and his team also deliver high-touch internal assessment and development efforts to top executives. He has previously held VP positions in both talent management and organization development at PepsiCo, and during the past seventeen years he has designed and delivered many of the company's world-class processes and tools. Prior to PepsiCo he worked as a consultant in organizational development for W. Warner Burke Associates and at IBM in the Communications Measurement and Corporate Personnel Research departments. Allan has served as chair of the Mayflower Group and on the SIOP executive board. He currently serves on the executive committee of The Conference Board's Council of Talent Management and on the board of directors for Human Resource People & Strategy (HRPS), the executive network of SHRM. He is an adjunct assistant professor at Teachers College, Columbia University and associate editor of the *Journal of Applied Behavioral Science*. He serves on the editorial boards of *Consulting Psychology Journal, Industrial-Organizational Psychology: Perspectives on Science*, the *Journal of Psychology and Business*, the *Journal of Social Psychology, People & Strategy*, and *OD Practitioner*. An active writer, he has authored several books, over thirty-five book chapters, and over one hundred and fifty practitioner and scholarly articles. Allan received his PhD in organizational psychology from Columbia University. He is a fellow of the Society for Industrial-Organizational Psychology, the American Psychological Association, and the Association for Psychological Science.